This book belongs to:

Name

_____

_____

School

_____

_____

Full Name	Age & Birthday

 **ABOUT ME**

Today I am....

☐ Happy   ☐ Bubbly   ☐ Tickled   ☐ Joyous

QUESTIONS	ANSWERS
Hair Color	
Eye Color	
Height	
Where were you born?	
Do you have any pets?	
What is your favorite food(s)?	
Do you have any brothers and sisters?	

What do you want to be when you grow up?

What is your favorite subject in school?

What do you like to do in your free time?

What makes
you unique? _____

First, read the entire passage. After that, go back and fill in the blanks. You can skip the blanks you're unsure about and finish them later.

entire	~~brag~~	~~persuade~~	~~grin~~	dream
bike	~~friendships~~	~~walk~~	~~opening~~	important

Hello, my name is Timmy! I've always found it challenging to make friends, to the point of anxiety. People find it difficult to believe, but I used to __walk__ around school by myself. I wanted to meet people, make friends, and have others show interest in me, but it just didn't happen. I was a good kid. I was intriguing. I was prepared to make new friends, but I couldn't make the other kids notice me. I was approaching everything incorrectly. I spent all of my energy attempting to __persuade__ other students that I was interesting. But, when I realized that trying to pique the interest of others in me was pointless, I changed my behavior. Being interested in others was the key to __opening__ the door to making friends for me. As a result of this, I was able to connect with children much more quickly. I made more good friends in a few weeks than I had in all of my previous school years combined.

SIMLE (Smile) ✓

A smile may appear to be such a simple thing to do, but it can open the path to a lot of good __friendships__. It is difficult to walk around with a smile on your face if you are in a situation where you are not making friends, no matter how hard you try. However, not smiling can make you feel even more out of place.

Now, I'm not suggesting that you walk around with a __grin__ on your face all day because people will think you're weird. But I'm talking about lightening up and sending out positive energy. Laugh at your classmates' jokes (even if they aren't funny) and smile at people as you pass by. You have a much better chance of making friends if you let people in a little.

LISTEN

Everyone wishes to be heard. It's easy to believe that the best way to make friends is to __brag__ about how cool you are. Doesn't this involve talking about yourself to others? Actually, no, it doesn't. It consists of being a part of a group, and listening to others is a big part. All of this is a natural part of maturing. When you were three, you could walk into a room and start talking, and everyone would stop and listen. But you no longer have that power. If you walk into a room full of your peers and begin bragging about how great you are, they will almost certainly tune you out.

FEEL IMPORTANT

Everyone wants to feel like they are the most _____ person in the room. It is a natural process that occurs to all of us. There's nothing wrong with feeling that way. When someone pays attention to you, you feel ten feet tall and walk around all day with a smile on your face and a spring in your step (remember that). You must be able to convey this feeling to others. If this makes you happy, know that it will make others happy as well.

I used to _____ about being so well-known that I didn't have time to do anything other than saying "hi" to people as I walked by. Just consider that for a moment. What's the point of that? Making friends involves not only "knowing a lot of people," but also "spending quality time with people."

You will have a much happier school life if you have a few good friends rather than a tight connection to the _____ school. What you are interested in is reflected in your friends. You grow together and share beautiful experiences that you will remember for months or years to come. Having close friends has a real impact on your life. The power of a few good friends is a thousand times greater than the power of 500 social media connections.

Knowing who you allow you to be yourself. Perhaps you enjoy watching silly stuff on YouTube, riding your _____, or cooking Tacos every Tuesday. My point is, don't pretend to be someone you're not just to fit in. You might miss out on a friendship with someone who shares your interests.

Extra Credit: Answer These 2 questions:

1. What are 3 ways to make friends?

2. What is the difference between acquaintance and friend?

Step 1: Double-check that the bottom numbers (the denominators) are the same.
Step 2: Add the top numbers (the numerators), then place that answer over the denominator

Visually Adding Simple Fractions

1)

$$\frac{3}{11} \quad + \quad \frac{4}{11} \quad = \quad \frac{7}{11}$$

2)

$$\frac{1}{10} \quad + \quad \frac{6}{10} \quad = \quad \underline{\quad\quad}$$

3)

$$\frac{4}{11} \quad + \quad \frac{5}{11} \quad = \quad \underline{\quad\quad}$$

4)

$$\frac{3}{12} \quad + \quad \frac{6}{12} \quad = \quad \underline{\quad\quad}$$

5)

$$\frac{1}{4} \quad + \quad \frac{2}{4} \quad = \quad \underline{\quad\quad}$$

Step 1: Double-check that the bottom numbers (the denominators) are the same.
Step 2: Add the top numbers (the numerators), then place that answer over the denominator
Step 3: Reduce the fraction to its simplest form (if possible)

Score : _____

Date : _____

Adding Fractions

1) $\dfrac{5}{7} + \dfrac{4}{7} = \dfrac{9}{7} = 1\dfrac{2}{7}$

2) $\dfrac{2}{8} + \dfrac{5}{8} =$

3) $\dfrac{6}{7} + \dfrac{4}{7} =$

4) $\dfrac{5}{4} + \dfrac{3}{4} =$

5) $\dfrac{1}{8} + \dfrac{3}{8} =$

6) $\dfrac{2}{6} + \dfrac{5}{6} =$

7) $\dfrac{2}{6} + \dfrac{2}{6} =$

8) $\dfrac{5}{4} + \dfrac{3}{4} =$

9) $\dfrac{8}{8} + \dfrac{6}{8} =$

10) $\dfrac{3}{7} + \dfrac{5}{7} =$

11) $\dfrac{7}{9} + \dfrac{1}{9} =$

12) $\dfrac{3}{9} + \dfrac{6}{9} =$

13) $\dfrac{2}{7} + \dfrac{4}{7} =$

14) $\dfrac{3}{6} + \dfrac{2}{6} =$

15) $\dfrac{3}{6} + \dfrac{5}{6} =$

The factors of a number are the numbers that add up to the original number when multiplied together. Factors of 8, for example, could be 2 and 4 because 2 * 4 equals 8.

Find the Greatest Common Factor for each number pair.

1)   15 , 3   __3__

2)   24 , 12   _____

3)   10 , 4   _____

4)   40 , 4   _____

5)   8 , 40   _____

6)   10 , 4   _____

7)   12 , 20   _____

8)   5 , 20   _____

9)   8 , 2   _____

10) 24 , 40   _____

11) 6 , 8   _____

12) 10 , 3   _____

13) 8 , 6   _____

14) 24 , 10   _____

15) 24 , 12   _____

16) 40 , 24   _____

17) 8 , 10   _____

18) 10 , 20   _____

19) 2 , 3   _____

20) 6 , 12   _____

Step 1: List or write ALL the factors of each number.

Step 2: Identify the common factors.

Step 3: After identifying the common factors, select or choose the number which has the largest value. This number will be your Greatest Common Factor (GCF).

Example:
12, 18

Factors of 12: 1, 2, 3, 4, 6, 12
Factors of 18: 1, 2, 3, 6, 9, 18

What is the Greatest Common Factor?
The GCF of 12 and 18 is 6. That's it!

The factors of a number are the numbers that add up to the original number when multiplied together. Factors of 8, for example, could be 2 and 4 because 2 * 4 equals 8.

List All of the Prime Factors for each number.

1) 38   **2, 19** _____

2) 49   _____

3) 35   _____

4) 25   _____

5) 15   _____

6) 44   _____

7) 32   _____

8) 48   _____

9) 22   _____

10) 21   _____

11) 30   _____

12) 20   _____

13) 39   _____

14) 14   _____

15) 12   _____

16) 26   _____

17) 46   _____

18) 40   _____

19) 24   _____

20) 10   _____

The term "prime factorization" refers to the process of determining which prime numbers multiply to produce the original number.

Score : _____

Date : _____

Step 1 : Divide the given number in two factors.

Step 2 : Now divide these two factors into other two multiples.

Step 3 : Repeat the step 2 until we reach all prime factors.

Step 4 : All the prime factors so obtained collectively known as prime factors

of given number. In order to cross check; multiply all the prime factors, you

must get the given number.

Find the Prime Factors of the Numbers

1)

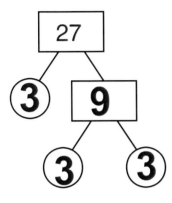

Prime Factors

_ X _ X _ = 27

2)

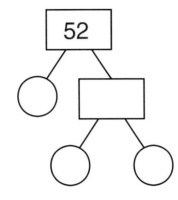

Prime Factors

_ X _ X _ = 52

3)

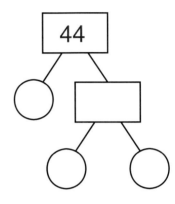

Prime Factors

_ X _ X _ = 44

4)

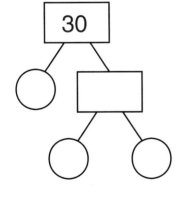

Prime Factors

_ X _ X _ = 30

5)

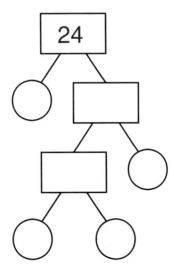

Prime Factors

_ X _ X _ X _ = 24

6)

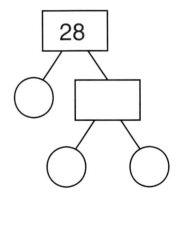

Prime Factors

_ X _ X _ = 28

Numerical Cognition Exercise
Rearranging Digits

Rearrange each set of numbers to produce the largest possible number.

1) 399   **993**   6) 846   _____

2) 744   _____   7) 844   _____

3) 488   _____   8) 345   _____

4) 616   _____   9) 959   _____

5) 734   _____   10) 559   _____

Rearrange each set of numbers to make the smallest number possible.

1) 897   **789**   6) 149   _____

2) 696   _____   7) 862   _____

3) 825   _____   8) 212   _____

4) 135   _____   9) 557   _____

5) 751   _____   10) 675   _____

Numerical Cognition Exercise
Rearranging Digits

Rearrange each set of numbers to produce the largest possible number.

1)   1,182   **8,211**_____

2)   1,549   _____

3)   5,366   _____

4)   3,869   _____

5)   2,853   _____

6)   7,769   _____

7)   7,521   _____

8)   8,146   _____

9)   8,161   _____

10)   7,769   _____

Rearrange each set of numbers to make the smallest number possible.

1)   7,816   **1,678**_____

2)   3,827   _____

3)   4,946   _____

4)   5,938   _____

5)   1,627   _____

6)   6,636   _____

7)   8,176   _____

8)   9,222   _____

9)   2,172   _____

10)   5,366   _____

TIME

Score : _____

Date : _____

What time is on the clock? _____

What time was it 1 hour ago? _____

What time was it 3 hours and 40 minutes ago? _____

What time will it be in 4 hours and 20 minutes? _____

What time is on the clock? _____

What time was it 2 hours ago? _____

What time will it be in 3 hours ? _____

What time will it be in 4 hours and 20 minutes? _____

What time is on the clock? _____

What time was it 1 hour ago? _____

What time was it 3 hours and 20 minutes ago? _____

What time will it be in 2 hours ? _____

What time is on the clock? _____

What time will it be in 3 hours and 20 minutes? _____

What time was it 2 hours ago? _____

What time was it 1 hour ago? _____

3rd Grade Grammar: Homophones vs Homographs vs. Homonyms

Score: _____

Date:_____

How do you know which 'there,' 'their,' or 'they're' to use when you're writing? Isn't it a difficult one? These words sound similar but have completely different meanings.

Words with the same sound but different meanings are referred to as **homophones**. Homophones can be spelled differently or the same way. Rose (the flower), rose (the past tense of 'rise,' and rows (a line of items or people) are all homophones.

Homographs are two or more words that have the same spelling but different meanings and it **doesn't have to sound the same**. Because homographs are words with multiple meanings, how can you tell which one is being used? Readers can determine which form of a homograph is being used by looking for context clues, or words surrounding it that provide information about the definition. Take a look at these homograph examples.

A **bat** is either a piece of sporting equipment or an animal.
Bass is either a type of fish or a musical genre.
A **pen** is a writing instrument or a small enclosure in which animals are kept.
Lean is a word that means to be thin or to rest against something.
A **skip** is a fictitious jump or missing out on something.

Homonyms are words that have the same spelling or pronunciation but different meanings. These words can be perplexing at times, especially for students learning to spell them. For example, right means moral, the opposite of left, and a personal freedom. Homonyms can refer to both homophones and homographs. Both a homograph and a homophone are included in the definition of a homonym. For example, the words 'bear,' 'tear,' and 'lead' are all homographs, but they also meet the criteria for homonyms. They simply have to have the same look or sound. Similarly, while the words 'sell,' 'cell,' 'by,' and 'buy' are all homophones, they are also homonyms.

1. **'there,' 'their,' or 'they're' are examples of _____.**
   a. Homophones
   b. Homographs

2. **_____ are words that have the same spelling or pronunciation but different meanings.**
   a. Homonyms
   b. Hemograms

3. **Choose the correct homophone for this sentence: Please don't drop and _____ that bottle of hand sanitizer!**
   a. brake
   b. break

4. **Homographs are two or more words that have the same spelling but different _____.**
   a. ending sounds
   b. meanings

5. **Current (A flow of water / Up to date) is both homograph and homophone.**
   a. True
   b. False

6. **To, two, and too are _____.**
   a. Homonyms
   b. Homagraphs

7. **The candle filled the _____ with a delicious scent.**
   a. air
   b. heir

8. **Kim drove _____ the tunnel.**
   a. threw
   b. through

9. John wants to go to _____ house for dinner, but they don't like her, so _____ going to say no.
   a. there, they're
   b. their, they're

10. We won a $95,000 _____!
    a. check
    b. cheque

11. For example, a pencil is not really made with _____.
    a. led
    b. lead

12. Choose the correct homophone for this sentence: Timmy was standing _____ in line.
    a. fourth
    b. forth

13. Homophones are two words that sound the same but have a different meanings.
    a. True
    b. False

14. The word ring in the following two sentences is considered what? She wore a ruby ring. | We heard the doorbell ring.
    a. hologram
    b. homograph

15. A Homograph is a word that has more than one meaning and doesn't have to sound the same.
    a. True
    b. False

16. Homophones occur when there are multiple ways to spell the same sound.
    a. True
    b. False

17. Select the correct homophone: I have very little (patience/patients) when students do not follow directions.
    a. patience
    b. patients

18. The correct homophone (s) are used in the sentence: Personally, I hate the smell of read meet.
    a. True
    b. False

19. The correct homophone(s) is used in the sentence: We saw a herd of cattle in the farmer's field.
    a. True
    b. False

20. What is NOT an example of a homograph?
    a. or, oar
    b. live, live

21. I love my _____ class.
    a. dear
    b. deer

22. We will go _____ after we finish our lesson.
    a. there
    b. their

23. Please grab _____ jacket for recess.
    a. you're
    b. your

24. There is _____ more water at the concession stand.
    a. no
    b. know

Grammar: Personal Pronouns

Pronouns are words that are used to rename, stand-in for, refer to, or rename nouns (a person, place, thing, or idea). As a result, they frequently behave exactly like nouns in a sentence. Pronouns allow a speaker or writer to change how they refer to a noun, so pronouns are limited in meaning to the noun they are referring to. For instance, if someone is telling a story about a friend named Jim and says, "He went to the store," he is referring to Jim.

Without pronouns, relating information in writing or speech would feel stiff and repetitive. Assume an author wanted to write a story about a young man named Mike. Without pronouns, the author would have to refer to Mike by his first name or as "the boy." The plot could go something like this:

"Mike awoke at 8:30 a.m. every day. Mike dressed for the day, and then the boy ate breakfast. "Mike was always late for school."

Take note of how repetitive the story becomes when pronouns are removed. However, if pronouns are used instead of nouns, the story becomes less repetitive and wooden. As an example:

"Mike awoke at 8:30 a.m. every day. He put on his day's clothes and then ate breakfast. "He was always late for school."

The most well-known type of pronoun is the personal pronoun, which is used to identify oneself, people being spoken to, and people being spoken about. Personal pronouns have traditionally been classified as either subjective or objective, singular or plural, and first, second, or third person, as shown below.

First-person, singular -- I, my, mine, me.

Second person, singular -- you, your, yours.

Third-person, singular -- he, his, him, she, her, hers, it, its.

First-person, plural -- we, our, ours, us.

Second person, plural -- your, yours.

Third person, plural -- they, their, theirs, them

In short, personal pronouns are grammar's stunt doubles; they stand-in for the people (and possibly animals) who appear in our sentences. They allow us to speak and write more efficiently because they prevent us from repeating cumbersome proper nouns all day.

1. **Pronouns stand-in for the people and _____.**
   a. animals
   b. nothing at all

2. **Using pronouns allows a speaker or writer to vary how they refer to a _____.**
   a. adverb
   b. noun

3. **The tie is very special. ___ is a magic tie.**
   a. He
   b. It

4. **Charlie and I went to a pond. _____saw two frogs.**
   a. They
   b. We

5. The turtle is tired. _____ is rest under the tree.
   a. Him
   b. It

6. Tim and I saw the lion in the jungle. ____were very afraid.
   a. Their
   b. We

7. The rabbit escaped from the trap and ran away. _____was safe.
   a. They
   b. It

8. The farmer's wife saw a wolf. _____shouted to the farmer for help.
   a. She
   b. It

9. The boys found a magic chain. _____gave it to the queen.
   a. They
   b. He

10. _____20 years old.
    a. Them
    b. She's

11. _____house is big.
    a. He
    b. His

12. _____name's Farah.
    a. Her
    b. She

13. How old is she?
    a. He's seven.
    b. She's seven.

14. What's his name?
    a. His name's Ali.
    b. Her name's Ali.

15. Mia and Omar enjoy listening to Ree's singing. Becomes:
    a. Them enjoy listening to Ree's singing.
    b. They enjoy listening to Ree's singing.

16. Dana kicked the ball. Becomes:
    a. She kicked the ball.
    b. He kicked the ball.

17. The dog is barking. _____ is barking at someone.
    a. He
    b. It

18. My sister likes basketball. _____ plays everyday.
    a. She
    b. He

3rd Grade Grammar: Contractions

Score: _____

Date: _____

Take a moment to visualize the process of blowing up a balloon. It grows larger and larger. When we let the air out, it shrinks or contracts. To contract means to shrink, reduce or get smaller.

In writing, a contraction is a word that combines two words to form a shorter word. In other words, the contraction makes the two words smaller. A contraction is simply a word that is a shortened form of two words combined.

When the words can and not are combined, the contraction word can't is formed. The apostrophe (as in this symbol: ') is a small punctuation mark that replaces the letters that have been removed. The apostrophe replaces the 'n' and the 'o' of not in can't.

		A	B	C	D
1.	_____	he'd	ha'd	hh'd	hp'd
2.	_____	yoo'rre	yoo're	you'rre	you're
3.	_____	wesn't	wassn't	wascn't	wasn't
4.	_____	sied	mhod	sha'd	she'd
5.	_____	they'll	thay'l	they'l	thay'll
6.	_____	aran't	arran't	aren't	arren't
7.	_____	let's	latt's	lett's	lat's
8.	_____	lad	I's	I'd	wts
9.	_____	she'l	sha'l	she'll	sha'll
10.	_____	wa'e	wa've	wa'va	we've
11.	_____	yoo'd	yood	yuo'd	you'd
12.	_____	ha'l	ha'll	he'l	he'll
13.	_____	I've	I'vw	Ikva	I'va
14.	_____	hesn't	hassn't	hascn't	hasn't
15.	_____	thai'd	thay'd	they'd	thei'd
16.	_____	you'll	yoo'll	you'l	yoo'l
17.	_____	haven'tt	havan't	haven't	havan'tt
18.	_____	wa'll	we'l	wa'l	we'll
19.	_____	yoo've	yoo'e	yuo've	you've
20.	_____	hadn't	hedn't	hedn'tt	hadn'tt
21.	_____	havan'tt	haven'tt	haven't	havan't

3rd Grade Grammar:
Contractions Sentence Building

Contracted words, also known as contractions, are short words formed by combining two words. In the contraction, letters are omitted and replaced with an apostrophe. The apostrophe indicates where the letters would be if the words were written in its entirety.

Practice *sentence* building. *U*nscramble the words to form a complete sentence and CIRCLE the contraction in each sentence.

1. _____ coming to _____ party?

   your · Who's

2. He's not _____ _____ us.

   with · coming

3. Aren't _____ _____ friend?

   you · Caroline's

4. __ wouldn't _____ in there if __ were _____

   you. · I · go · I

5. _____ ready for __ vacation.

   I'm · a

6. He's _____ to _____ for the _____

   Florida · going · holiday.

7. _____ staying in _____

   We're · town.

8. _____ _____ at the moment.

   They're · undecided

9. _____ see you next _____

   I'll · week.

10. _____ going for __ walk.

I'm   a

11. It's freezing _____

outside!

12. __ _____ _____ my glasses anywhere.

I   find   can't

13. I _____ have _____ ____ much!

so   shouldn't   eaten

14. _____ the time?

What's

15. Where's ____ newspaper?

my

16. _____ your wedding?

When's

17. Let's go to _____ _____

the   store.

18. I'm ready ____ ____ now.

go   to

19. You're _____ ____ come along.

welcome   to

20. I've _____ to _____ _____ already.

store   the   been

21. He isn't planning ____ _____ _____

along.   to   come

22. _____ hasn't made ____ her _____ yet.

mind   up   She

3rd Grade Grammar:
SUPERLATIVE ADJECTIVES

A superlative adjective is a comparative adjective that describes something as being of the highest degree or extreme. When comparing three or more people or things, we use superlative adjectives. Superlative adjectives typically end in 'est'. Examples of superlative adjectives include the words biggest and fastest.

Unscramble Word Tip: Try solving the easy words first, and then go back and answer the more difficult ones.

prettiest	hottest	crowded	friendliest	biggest	smallest
saddest	best	worst	tallest	shortest	longest
fattest	newest	heaviest	nicest	beautiful	expensive
cheapest	comfortable	youngest	largest		

1. peehtsac   _ h _ a _ _ _ _

2. talresg   _ _ _ _ e s _

3. ntogels   _ o n _ _ _ _

4. wsenet   n e _ _ _ _

5. icetns   n _ _ _ s _

6. tstosreh   _ _ _ r _ _ _ t

7. samlsetl   _ _ _ _ l _ _ t

8. lstteal   _ a _ _ e _ _

9. goysunte   _ _ _ n _ _ s _

10. tggsbie   _ _ _ g _ s _

11. eftastt   _ _ t _ _ _ t

12. ttoesht   h _ _ _ e _ _

13. adstdes   _ _ d _ _ s _

14. filtaubeu   _ _ a _ _ _ _ _ l

15. ctlefarbmoo   _ _ _ _ _ r _ a b _ _

16. ddrwoce   _ _ _ _ _ e d

17. enpsvxeei   e _ _ _ n _ _ _ _

18. esdeirfiltn   _ r _ _ _ _ l _ _ s _

19. hitvseea   h _ _ _ _ _ _ _ t

20. espttriet   _ r _ _ _ i _ _ _

21. bets   _ _ s _

22. wrsot   _ _ _ s _

3rd Grade History: Thomas Edison

First, read the entire passage. After that, go back and fill in the blanks. You can skip the blanks you're unsure about and finish them later.

devices	teacher	dedicated	research	Morse
passed	hearing	invented	light	dream

Thomas Alva Edison was born in Milan, Ohio, on February 11, 1847. He developed _____ loss at a young age. He was a creative and inquisitive child. However, he struggled in school, possibly because he couldn't hear his _____. He was then educated at home by his mother.

Because of his numerous important inventions, Thomas Edison was nicknamed the "wizard." On his own or in collaboration with others, he has designed and built more than 1,000 _____. The phonograph (record player), the lightbulb, and the motion-picture projector are among his most notable inventions.

Although Thomas did not invent the first electric _____ bulb, he did create the first practical electric light bulb that could be manufactured and used in the home. He also _____ other items required to make the light bulb usable in homes, such as safety fuses and on/off switches for light sockets.

As a teenager, Thomas worked as a telegraph operator. Telegraphy was one of the most important communication systems in the country at the time. Thomas was skilled at sending and receiving _____ code messages. He enjoyed tweaking with telegraphic instruments, and he came up with several improvements to make them even better. By early 1869, he had left his telegraphy job to pursue his _____ of becoming a full-time inventor.

Edison worked tirelessly with scientists and other collaborators to complete projects. He established _____ facilities in Menlo Park, California, and West Orange, New Jersey. Finally, Edison established companies that manufactured and sold his successful inventions.

Edison's family was essential to him, even though he spent the majority of his life _____ to his work. He had six children from two marriages. Edison _____ away on October 18, 1931.

3rd Grade History: Christopher Columbus

When Christopher Columbus discovered America, he set in motion centuries of transatlantic colonization. He was an Italian explorer.

Christopher Columbus made four trips across the Atlantic Ocean from Spain in 1492, 1493, 1498, and 1502. He was adamant about finding a direct water route west from Europe to Asia, but he never succeeded. Instead, he discovered the Americas. Though he did not "discover" the so-called New World—millions of people already lived there—his voyages marked the start of centuries of exploration and colonization of North and South America.

With three ships: the Nina, the Pinta, and the Santa Maria, Columbus, and his crew set sail from Spain on August 3, 1492. The ships arrived in the Bahamas on October 12, not in the East Indies, as Columbus had assumed, but on one of the Bahamian islands, most likely San Salvador.

Columbus sailed from island to island in what is now known as the Caribbean for months, looking for the "pearls, precious stones, gold, silver, spices, and other objects and merchandise whatsoever" that he had promised his Spanish patrons, but he didn't find much. In January 1493, he set sail for Spain, leaving several dozen men behind in a makeshift settlement on Hispaniola (present-day Haiti and the Dominican Republic).

During his first voyage, he kept a detailed diary. Christopher Columbus' journal was written between August 3, 1492, and November 6, 1492, and it describes everything from the wildlife he saw, such as dolphins and birds, to the weather and the moods of his crew.

Circle the correctly spelled word.

	A	B	C	D
1.	America	Amerryca	Ameryca	Amerrica
2.	spices	spicesc	spises	spicess
3.	Eurropaen	European	Europaen	Eurropean
4.	coast	coasct	cuast	coasst
5.	abrroad	abruad	abroad	abrruad
6.	sailor	siallor	saillor	sialor
7.	nations	nattions	nascons	natsions
8.	explurers	explorers	expllorers	expllurers
9.	sylver	syllver	sillver	silver
10.	Spayn	Spian	Spyan	Spain
11.	Indains	Indainss	Indianss	Indians
12.	discover	disssover	disscover	dissover
13.	islend	iscland	island	issland

3rd Grade History Reading Comprehension: Walt Disney

First, read the article. After that, go back and fill in the blanks. You can skip the blanks you're unsure about and finish them later. Don't try to do it all at one time. Break it down so that it's "do-able" and not so overwhelming. Take your time. Ask questions. Get help if you need it.

Mickey	Donald	sister	Hollywood	art
Red	Chicago	newspaper	friends	train
four	entertainment	White	Alice	Peter
Club	snacks	vacation	brother	theme

On December 5, 1901, Walter Elias Disney was born in _____, Illinois. His family relocated to a farm outside of Marceline, Missouri, when he was _____ years old, thanks to his parents, Elias and Flora. Walt loved growing up on the farm with his three older brothers (Herbert, Raymond, and Roy) and younger _____ (Ruth). Walt discovered his passion for drawing and art in Marceline.

The Disneys relocated to Kansas City after four years in Marceline. On weekends, Walt continued to draw and attend _____ classes. He even bartered his drawings for free haircuts with a local barber. Walt got a summer job on a train. On the _____, he walked back and forth, selling _____ and newspapers. Walt had a great time on the train and would be fascinated by trains for the rest of his life.

Walt's family relocated to Chicago around the time he started high school. Walt studied at the Chicago Art Institute and worked as a cartoonist for the school _____. Walt decided at the age of sixteen that he wanted to fight in World War I. Due to the fact that he was still too young to join the army, he decided to drop out of school and join the _____ Cross instead. He spent the next year in France driving ambulances for the Red Cross.

Disney returned from the war eager to launch his artistic career. He began his career in an art studio and later moved on to an advertising firm. During this time, he met artist Ubbe Iwerks and became acquainted with animation.

Walt aspired to create his own animated cartoons. He founded his own company, Laugh-O-Gram. He sought the help of some of his _____, including Ubbe Iwerks. They made animated cartoons that were only a few minutes long. Despite the popularity of the cartoons, the business did not make enough money, and Walt was forced to declare bankruptcy.

Disney, on the other hand, was not going to be deterred by a single setback. In 1923, he relocated to _____, California, and founded the Disney Brothers' Studio with his _____ Roy. He enlisted the services of Ubbe Iwerks and a number of other animators once more. They created the well-known character Oswald the Lucky Rabbit. The company was a success. However, Universal Studios acquired the Oswald trademark and hired all of Disney's animators except Ubbe Iwerks.

Walt had to start all over again. This time, he came up with a new character called _____ Mouse. He made the first animated film with sound. Steamboat Willie was the title of the film, which starred Mickey and Minnie Mouse. Walt provided the voices for Steamboat Willie. The movie was a huge success. Disney kept working, creating new characters like _____ Duck, Goofy, and Pluto. With the release of the cartoon Silly Symphonies and the first color animated film, Flowers and Trees, he had even more success.

In 1932, Walt Disney decided to create a full-length animated film called Snow _____. People thought he was insane for attempting to create such a long cartoon. The film was dubbed "Disney's folly." However, Disney was confident that the film would be a success. The film, which was released in 1937, took five years to complete. The film was a huge box office success, becoming the most successful film of 1938.

Disney used the proceeds from Snow White to establish a film studio and produce other animated films such as Pinocchio, Fantasia, Dumbo, Bambi, _____ in Wonderland, and _____ Pan. During WWII, Disney's film production slowed as he worked on training and propaganda films for the United States government. Following the war, Disney began to produce live-action films alongside animated films. Treasure Island was his first major live-action film.

Television was a new technology that was taking off in the 1950s. Disney wished to be a part of the television industry as well. Disney's Wonderful World of Color, the Davy Crockett series, and the Mickey Mouse _____ was among the first Disney television shows to air on network television.

Disney, who is constantly coming up with new ideas, had the idea to build a _____ park featuring rides and entertainment based on his films. In 1955, Disneyland opened its doors. It cost $17 million to construct. Although it wasn't an immediate success, Disney World has since grown into one of the world's most popular _____ destinations. Walt Disney World, a much larger park in Florida, would be built later by Disney. He contributed to the plans but passed away before the park opened in 1971.

Disney died of lung cancer on December 15, 1966. His legacy endures to this day. Every year, millions of people enjoy his films and theme parks. Every year, his company continues to produce fantastic films and _____.

3rd Grade Reading
Comprehension Multiple Choice:
Walt Disney

Make sure you go back and read the Disney article through to the very end. If you attempt to complete this assignment solely by scanning for answers, you will almost certainly pick the incorrect answer. Take your time. Ask questions. Get help if you need it. Good Luck!

1. Walter Elias Disney was born in Chicago, ____.
   a. Illinois
   b. Italy

2. Walter's parents names were Elias and Flora.
   a. True
   b. False

3. Walt got a summer job on a _____.
   a. train
   b. boat

4. Walt's younger sister name was ____.
   a. Ruby
   b. Ruth

5. Walt had _____ brothers.
   a. three
   b. two

6. In 1923, walt relocated to Hollywood, _____.
   a. Colorado
   b. California

7. Steamboat ____ was the title of the film, which starred Mickey and Minnie Mouse.
   a. William
   b. Willie

8. Walt spent the next year in France driving _____ for the Red Cross.
   a. taxi cabs
   b. ambulances

9. Walt and his friends created the well-known character Oswald the Lucky _____t.
   a. Dog
   b. Rabbi

10. Walt's first color animated film was____.
    a. Bears and Tigers
    b. Flowers and Trees

11. In ____, Disneyland opened its doors.
    a. 1955
    b. 1995

12. _____ was among the first Disney television shows to air on network television.
    a. Mickey Mouse Club
    b. Mickey and Friends

13. _____ was his first major live-action film.
    a. Treasure Island
    b. Treats Island

14. Walt Disney decided to create a full-length animated film called _____.
    a. Snow White
    b. Robin Hood

The History of the Calendar

Score: _____

Date: _____

Is there a calendar in your family's home? Every day, the majority of households use a calendar. Calendars help us stay organized. Using a calendar, you can keep track of the passing of time and plan ahead. The ancients based their calendars on the most apparent regular events they were aware of—the Sun, Moon, and stars changing positions. These calendars assisted them in determining when to plant and harvest their crops. Different groups of people developed other calendars over time based on their own needs and beliefs.

The Gregorian calendar is used by people all over the world. In 1752, the world switched to the Gregorian calendar. Otherwise, different calendars were used by people all over the world.

Julius Caesar first introduced the 12 months of the calendar as we know them today on January 1st, 45 BC.

The previous Roman calendar had the year begin in March and end in December. Romulus, Rome's legendary first king, had used it since 753 BC. Because it only accounted for 304 days in a year, this calendar was later modified.

To account for the missing days, Rome's second king, Numa Pompilius, added two months at the end of the calendar, Januarius and Februarius. He also put in place an intercalary month that fell after Februarius in some years. These years were nicknamed "leap years." In addition, he deleted one day from each month with 30 days, making them 29 days instead.

This resulted in 355 days in a regular year and 377 days in a leap year. The leap years were declared at the king's discretion. Despite its instability, the calendar was in use for 700 years.

However, it became highly perplexing because the seasons and calendars did not correspond. It wreaked havoc on the farmers.

So, in 45 BC, Julius Caesar, with the help of his astronomers, decided to change the calendar and make it more stable. The seasons finally had a chance to catch up.

Since 1752, when the Gregorian calendar was adopted worldwide to synchronize it with the English and American colonies, the same calendar had been in use. Since Caesar's time, the world and its boundaries have expanded dramatically! The Gregorian calendar corrected the Julian calendar error of calculating one revolution of the earth around the sun to account for 365.2422 days.

That's all there is to it! Julius Caesar was the first to institute the 12-month calendar we have today!

Calendar Words Unscramble

Name: _____

Date: _____

Unscramble the days and months below.

August	November	Monday	May	April	June
Friday	March	January	September	October	July
Saturday	February	December	Sunday	Thursday	Tuesday
Wednesday					

1. nuayraj — January

2. beyuarrf — February

3. mrach — March

4. arilp — April

5. amy — May

6. njeu — June

7. yjlu — July

8. uasutg — August

9. beermstpe — September

10. borotec — October

11. rmnbeveo — November

12. edebemrc — December

13. oymdna — Monday

14. styaued — Tuesday

15. ydsaeedwn — Wednesday

16. hrtydasu — Thursday

17. dfiray — Friday

18. srtduaay — Saturday

19. saduny — Sunday

3rd Grade Health Spelling
Words: Healthy Routines

Write the correct word for each sentence.

Reading	overeat	Eating	read	fat
fresh	fruit	health	glass	chair
floss	Breakfast	Staying	daily	Sleep
fiber	enough	burn	Walking	body

1. Creating a healthy _daily_ routine is simple.

2. _Staying_ hydrated is vital for our health.

3. Exercise has tremendous _health_ benefits.

4. Exposure to the sun enables the _____ to produce vitamin D.

5. _Walking_ is one of the most underrated healthy habits you can do.

6. Vegetables are low in calories, yet high in vitamins, minerals, and _fiber_.

7. _Eating_ has benefits to both your physical and mental health.

8. _Sleep_ is the only time during the day where our bodies are able to relax, unwind and recover.

9. _____ a variety of good foods.

10. _____ is the most important meal of the day.

11. Drink a _____ of water.

12. Sitting in your _____ all day long isn't good for you.

13. Excess body _____ comes from eating more than we need.

14. Cooking the right amount makes it easier to not _____.

15. Physical activity helps us _____ off the extra calories.

16. Eat _____ instead of eating a candy bar.

17. Make time to _____ every day.

18. Don't forget to _____.

19. Swap sugary desserts for _____ fruit.

20. Get _____ sleep.

3rd Grade Spelling Words
Unscramble

Unscramble Word Tip: Try solving the easy words first, and then go back and answer the more difficult ones.

compare	group	pond	taught	laundry	start
grade	wrap	front	stone	pardon	city
shirt	open	am	value	office	hope
highest	close	person	verb	hear	near
travel	pencil				

1. lseoc   c _ _ _ _

2. oesnpr   _ _ _ _ o n

3. npdrao   _ _ _ d _ n

4. ma   a _

5. ntoes   _ _ _ _ e

6. earn   n _ _ _

7. ithrs   _ _ _ r _

8. auevl   _ a _ _ _

9. atelvr   t _ _ v _ _

10. poeh   _ _ p _

11. tciy   _ _ _ y

12. bvre   _ _ _ b

13. aehr   _ e _ _

14. ndpo   p _ _ _

15. tuahgt   t _ _ _ h _

16. adrge   _ _ _ _ e

17. ofrnt   _ _ o _ _

18. trats   s _ _ _ _

19. nydrual   _ a _ _ _ _ y

20. enpo   _ _ e _

21. wapr   _ _ _ p

22. ilencp   _ _ _ _ i l

23. gishteh   _ _ _ h _ s _

24. aempcro   _ o _ _ _ r _

25. orugp   _ r _ _ _

26. oeffic   _ f f _ _ _

3rd Grade Spelling Words Crossword

Score: _____

Date: _____

Complete the crossword by filling in a word that fits each clue. Fill in the correct answers, one letter per square, both across and down, from the given clues. There will be a gray space between multi-word answers.

Tip: Solve the easy clues first, and then go back and answer the more difficult ones.

Across

1. behave in a certain manner
4. a strong drive for success
8. hold on tightly
9. mentally quick and resourceful
10. protect against a challenge or attack
11. an impairment of health
13. physically weak
15. an object with a spherical shape
16. hold firmly

Down

1. take in a liquid
3. take into one's family
5. fearless and daring
6. coldness due to a cold environment
9. an organized group of workers
12. having unexpected good luck
14. move smoothly and effortlessly
17. propel with force
18. as far as something can go
19. a child's room for a baby

ABSORB   ADOPT   DISEASE
LIMIT   ACT   CLEVER
AMBITION   NURSERY   FRAIL
BOLD   DEFEND   CHILL
GLIDE   GRASP   FORTUNATE
GLOBE   LAUNCH   CREW
CLING

3rd Grade Science Spelling Words

Score: _____

Date: _____

Instructions: Match the science words to the correct meaning.

#		Word		Meaning	
1	☐	Shadow		Having magnetic properties	A
2	☐	Nectar		Study of earth	B
3	☐	Prey		A dark area	C
4	☐	Gas		Unicellular microorganism	D
5	☐	Mixture		Any true information	E
6	☐	Fossil		A coordinating organ of the human body	F
7	☐	Bacteria		A combination of different things	G
8	☐	Brain		A thin tube made up of glass	H
9	☐	Geology		The study of living beings	I
10	☐	Atom		The smallest particle	J
11	☐	Magnetic		Juicy fluid within flowers	K
12	☐	Dissolve		State of matter that can expand freely	L
13	☐	Fact		The remains of plant or animal	M
14	☐	Biology		Bony plates in the fish skin	N
15	☐	Organism		Kill and hunt for food	O
16	☐	Scale		Expression of heaviness	P
17	☐	Test tube		An individual/living being	Q
18	☐	Weigh		Solid form in any liquid	R

3rd Grade Storytime: Let Thy Hair Down

First, read the entire story. After that, go back and fill in the blanks. You can skip the blanks you're unsure about and finish them later.

small	loved	stronger	agreed	tower
climbed	condition	child	fresh	terrified

Once upon a time, there was a man and a woman who had long wished for a _____ in desperation. Finally, the woman hoped that God was about to grant her wish.

These people had a _____ window in the back of their house to see a beautiful garden. It was brimming with the most lovely flowers and herbs. It was, however, surrounded by a high wall, and no one dared to enter it because it belonged to a Witch, who wielded great power and was feared throughout the world.

One day, the woman was standing by this window, looking down into the garden, when she noticed a bed planted with the most beautiful rampion (rapunzel), and it looked so _____ and green that she wanted so badly for it and sought to eat some.

This desire grew _____ by the day, and because she knew she couldn't get any of it, she looked pale and miserable.

Then her husband became concerned and demanded to know, "What displeases you, dear Wife?

"Ah," she replied, "if I don't get some of the rampions in the garden behind our house to eat, I'll die."

"Rather than letting your wife die, bring her some of the rampions yourself; let it cost you what it will!" thought the man who _____ her.

In the late afternoon, he _____ over the wall into the Witch's garden, grabbed a handful of rampion, and hurriedly handed it to his wife. She immediately made herself a salad out of it and gobbled up it.

She, on the other hand, liked it so much-so much that she craved it three times as much the next day. Her husband had to return to the garden if he was to get any rest. As a result, in the bleakness of the evening, he let himself down once more. But when he got down the wall, he was _____ because he saw the Witch standing before him.

"How dare you come into my garden and steal my rampion like a thief?" she responded angrily. You will pay for it!"

"Ah, let mercy take the place of justice!" he replied. I had no choice but to do it. My wife saw your rampion from the window and craved it so much that she would have died if she hadn't gotten some to eat."

The Witch then softened her rage and said to him, "If the case is as you say, I will allow you to take as much rampion as you want, but there is one _____: you must give me the child that your wife will bring into the world." It will be well cared for, and I will look after it like a mother."

In his terror, the man _____ to everything, and when the woman finally had a little daughter, the Witch appeared immediately, gave the child the name Rapunzel, and took it away with her.

Rapunzel grew up to be the most beautiful child in the world. When she was twelve years old, the Witch locked her in a _____ in the middle of a forest with no stairs or door. But there was a small window at the very top. When the Witch desired to enter, she positioned herself beneath this and cried:

"Rapunzel, Rapunzel, let thy hair down."

3rd Grade Storytime: Let Thy Hair Down| Part 2

First, read the entire passage. After that, go back and fill in the blanks. You can skip the blanks you're unsure about and finish them later.

cut	years	dark	terrified	long
happily	tower	husband	escaped	separated
beloved	transport	sobbed	scissors	forest

Rapunzel had magnificent _____ hair as fine as spun gold, and when she heard the Witch's voice, she unfastened her long braided locks and wound them around one of the window hooks above. The hair then fell twenty ells down, and the Witch climbed up by it.

After a year or two, the King's Son rode through the forest and passed by the _____. Then he heard a song that was so lovely that he stopped and listened. This was Rapunzel, who spent her time alone, letting her sweet voice ripple outward.

The King's Son wanted to climb up to her and looked for the tower's door, but there was none to be found. He rode home, but the singing had touched him so deeply that he went out into the _____ every day to listen to it.

When he was standing behind a tree, he saw a Witch come by and heard her cry:

"Rapunzel, Rapunzel, let thy hair down."

Rapunzel then let down her hair braids, and the Witch climbed up to her.

"If that's the ladder by which one climbs up, I'll try my luck for a change," he said.

When it got _____ the next day, he went to the tower and cried:

"Rapunzel, Rapunzel, let thy hair down."

The hair instantly fell down, and the King's Son climbed up.

Rapunzel was _____ at first when a man her eyes had never seen before approached her. But the King's Son began to speak to her as if she were a friend, telling her that his heart had been so shaken that he couldn't sleep and that he had been forced to see her.

When he asked Rapunzel if she would take him as her _____ and she saw that he was young and handsome, she thought to herself, "He will love me more than old Dame Gothel does," and she said yes and laid her hand in his.

"I will gladly go away with you, but I don't know how to get down," she added. Bring a strand of silk with you every time you come, and I'll weave a ladder out of it. When that is completed, I will come down, and you will _____ me on your horse."

They agreed that he should come to her every evening until that time because the older woman came by day. The Witch did not comment until Rapunzel said to her, "Tell me, Dame Gothel, how it is that you are so much heavier for me to draw up than the young King's Son-he will be with me in a moment."

"You wicked child!" exclaimed the Witch. "What do you say!" I hear you say. I thought I'd _____ you from the rest of the world, but you've duped me!"

In her rage, she clutched Rapunzel's lovely locks, wrapped them twice around her left hand, grabbed a pair of _____ with her right, and snip, snap, they were cut off, and the lovely braids lay on the ground. And she was so pitiful that she banished Rapunzel to the desert, where she had to live in agony and misery.

However, on the same day that she cast out Rapunzel, the Witch, in the evening, glued the braids of hair she had _____ off to the window hook; and when the King's Son came and cried:

"Rapunzel, Rapunzel, Let down thy hair," she let the hair down.

The King's Son climbed. He did not see his _____ Rapunzel above but rather the Witch, who glared at him with wicked and cruel eyes.

"Aha!" she mocked, "you would fetch your dearest!" However, the lovely bird is no longer singing in the nest. The cat has it and will scratch your eyes out as well. Rapunzel is no longer yours! You'll never see her again!"

The King's Son was overcome with grief and jumped from the tower in sadness. He _____ with his life, but the thorns he landed on punctured his eyes. Then he wandered around the forest completely blind, eating only roots and berries and doing nothing but mourn and weep over the loss of his dearest wife.

So he wandered around in misery for a few _____ before arriving in the desert, where Rapunzel lived in misfortune. He heard a voice and went toward it because it sounded familiar. When he approached, Rapunzel recognized him and _____ on his neck. Two of her tears wetted his eyes, causing them to clear and allowing him to see as before.

He led her to his Kingdom, where he was joyfully received, and they lived _____ and merrily for a long time.

Score: _____

3rd Grade Geography Words

Date: _____

Instructions: Match the words to the correct meaning.

1	[ ]	Atlas		A coral reef or an island in the shape of a ring.	A
2	[ ]	Atoll		The study of the planet Earth's physical features.	B
3	[ ]	Altitude		A stream that flows into a large lake, or a river.	C
4	[ ]	Border		The half of a sphere. Hint: Northern and Southern___.	D
5	[ ]	Capital		The measure of the distance from the east or the west of Prime Meridian.	E
6	[ ]	Country		The measure of elevation above sea level.	F
7	[ ]	Desert		The 3rd planet of our solar system and the planet in which we all live.	G
8	[ ]	Earth		A narrow passage of water connecting two water bodies.	H
9	[ ]	Equator		A political state or a nation. For example, India, Thailand.	I
10	[ ]	Geography		The measure of the distance from the north or the south of the Equator.	J
11	[ ]	Glacier		A mass of ice that is slowly moving.	K
12	[ ]	Hemisphere		A collection of maps of the planet Earth.	L
13	[ ]	Latitude		A large area covered with sand, where water or vegetation is either very little or not present at all.	M
14	[ ]	Longitude		An artificial line drawn segregating two geographical areas.	N
15	[ ]	Meridian		A city exercising primary status and where the government is located.	O
16	[ ]	Plain		A piece of land on high ground.	P
17	[ ]	Plateau		A piece of land that is flat.	Q
18	[ ]	Strait		A line drawn on the center of the earth separating the north and south pole.	R
19	[ ]	Tributary		An imaginary circle passing through two poles.	S

3rd Grade Geography: Rivers

A river is a moving, flowing body of water. Typically, a river discharges its water into an ocean, lake, pond, or even another river. Rivers vary in size, and there is no hard and fast rule about how large a flow of water must be to be classified as a river. Rain, melting snow, lakes, ponds, and even glaciers can all contribute to river water. Rivers flow downhill from their headwaters. They are classified as freshwater biomes.

A river is a body of primarily freshwater that flows across the land's surface, usually traversing its way to the sea.

A river channel is a type of channel found in rivers.

All rivers flow in channels, and the bottom of the channel is known as the bed, while the sides are known as the banks.

When one stream meets another, they merge. The smaller stream is referred to as a tributary. A large number of tributaries form a river.

A river expands as it collects more and more water from its tributaries.

When a river comes to an end, it's known as the mouth.

Rivers provide us with food, energy, recreation, boating routes, and, of course, water for drinking and watering crops.

3 Longest Rivers:

The Nile River runs for 4,135 miles. It is found on the African continent, primarily in the countries of Egypt and Sudan. It flows into the Mediterranean Sea from the north.

The Amazon River stretches for 3,980 miles. It flows through several countries on the South American continent, including Brazil, Venezuela, Bolivia, and Ecuador. It comes to an end at the Atlantic Ocean.

The Mississippi River and Missouri River systems form the longest river system in North America.The Missouri River is a tributary of the Mississippi River. It is 6,279 kilometers long. It is a river that flows into the Gulf of Mexico.

Do you understand there is a difference between upstream and downstream? Upstream refers to the direction from which the water source originates, such as a mountain. Downstream refers to the direction in which the water flows to reach its final destination.

Fast Facts:

There are 76 rivers in the world that are more than 1000 miles long.

Many people believe that rivers always flow south, but four of the world's ten longest rivers flow north.

There are approximately 3.5 million miles of rivers in the United States alone.

1. **Rivers vary in _____.**
   a. height
   b. size

2. **A river is a moving, flowing _____ of water.**
   a. body
   b. streams

3. A river is a body of primarily _____ that flows across the land's surface.
   a. freshwater
   b. biome

4. When one stream meets another, they_____.
   a. cross over
   b. merge

5. When a river comes to an end, it's known as the _____.
   a. mouth
   b. lake

6. A large number of _____ form a river.
   a. tributaries
   b. oceans

7. A river expands as it _____ more and more water from its tributaries.
   a. collects
   b. decreases

8. The _____ runs for 4,135 miles.
   a. Nile River
   b. Mississippi River

9. _____ flows through several countries on the South American continent, including Brazil.
   a. Amazon River
   b. Antarctica River

10. _____ and _____ systems form the longest river system in North America.
   a. Mississippi River and Missouri River
   b. Mississippi River and Michigan River

Extra Credit: Answer The Following 3 Questions:

(1.) Where is majority of all water located on Earth?

(2.) What is all the water on earth called?

(3.) Why the Earth is called Blue planet?

_____

_____

_____

_____

_____

_____

_____

3rd Grade Science: Albert Einstein

First, read the entire passage. After that, go back and fill in the blanks. You can skip the blanks you're unsure about and finish them later.

mathematics	boat	Nobel	overnight	top
experiment	paper	books	Germany	failed
pocket	marriage	missed	socks	door

Albert Einstein was born in _____ on March 14, 1879. Because he was Jewish, he fled to the United States to avoid Hitler and the Second World War.

When his grandmother first saw him, she said he was stupid! Little did she know!

He apparently didn't speak until he was four years old, and even then, he would repeat words and sentences until he was seven.

His father gave him a simple _____ compass when he was about five years old, and it quickly became his favorite toy!

He became obsessed with magnetism, which is basically all about magnets and how they work, from that day forward.

Young Einstein didn't like the way his grammar school taught him. He also wasn't particularly fond of authority. As a result, he was expelled from school quite a few times.

He developed an interest in _____ and science at the age of seven.

When Einstein was about ten years old, a much older friend gave him a large stack of science, mathematics, and philosophy _____.

He'd published his first scientific _____ by the age of sixteen. That is absolutely incredible!

Numerous reports have shown that Einstein _____ math in school, but his family has stated that this is not the case. They claimed he was always at the _____ of his class in math and could solve some challenging problems. He was obsessed with geometry and algebra, and no one taught him anything – he taught himself! He was also constantly attempting to prove various mathematical theories on his own.

Yes, he was brilliant.

Although he was not a top student in every subject in school, he certainly made up for it when he and his family moved to Switzerland when he was older.

He began teaching math and physics in 1900.

Einstein was a little disorganized. So, if you're feeling the same way, don't despair; there is still hope!

As an adult, he frequently _____ appointments, and because his mind was all over the place, his lectures were a little difficult to understand.

He didn't wear _____ and had uncombed hair! Even at posh dinners, he'd arrive unkempt, with crumpled clothes and, of course, no socks!

Despite the fact that he was all over the place, a little shabby, and a little difficult to understand, he rocked the world with his Theory of Relativity in 1915. An _____ in 1919 proved the theory correct. He became famous almost _____, and he suddenly received invitations to travel worldwide, as well as honors from all over the world!

In 1921, he was awarded the _____ Prize for Physics. He'd come a long way from the boy who was told he'd never amount to anything!

Today, his other discoveries enabled us to have things like garage _____ openers, televisions, and DVD players. Time magazine named him "Person of the Century" in 1999.

One of his favorite activities was to take a _____ out on a lake and take his notebook with him to think and write everything down. Perhaps this is what inspired him to create his inventions!

Einstein's first _____ produced two sons. His daughter, Lierserl, is believed to have died when she was young. He married twice, and she died before him.

On April 18, 1955, the great scientist died in America.

3rd Grade Science: All About Beavers

Score: _____

Date: _____

First, read the entire passage. After that, go back and fill in the blanks. You can skip the blanks you're unsure about and finish them later.

hammer	growing	slow	building	wild
plants	fur	slap	underwater	rodents

Beavers are mammals well-known for their _____ abilities. Dams are built out of branches, stones, and mud. A dam stretches across a stream and blocks the flow of water. This results in a large pond. Beavers build their homes in these ponds' still waters rather than in rushing streams.

Beavers are _____, which are a type of animal. They have a kinship with mice, squirrels, and muskrats. Beavers are classified into two species or types. North America is home to the American beaver. The Eurasian beaver can be found in Europe and Asia. Beavers can be found in rivers, streams, and lakes. They spend some time on land as well.

Beavers have a total length of about 4 feet (1.3 meters), including the tail. Beavertails are scaly, flat, and paddle-shaped. Their stocky bodies and short legs are covered in thick brown fur. Beavers carry objects with their tiny front feet. Beavers are _____ on land, but their webbed back feet help them swim. Beavers can submerge for up to 15 minutes underwater.

Beavers are herbivores, which means they eat _____. They primarily consume tree buds, leaves, twigs, and the layer beneath the bark.

Beavers cut down young trees with their powerful jaws and teeth. The beaver's large front teeth never stop _____. The constant gnawing on wood by beavers helps to keep their teeth from growing too long.

They work in groups to construct dams. Beaver couples create lodges out of sticks and mud. A lodge can be up to 5 feet (1.5 meters) tall. It has a dome-shaped roof. Beavers are strong swimmers who can stay submerged for up to 15 minutes. Beavers have a translucent third eyelid (called a nictitating membrane) that covers and protects their eyes while still allowing some sight _____. Their ears and noses are valvular, which means they can close while diving underwater.

Even in the wee hours of the morning, Beavers have a hard time keeping their hands off the _____ They are prolific builders during the night.   As a result, they are "as busy as a beaver."

Beavers will _____ the water with their broad, scaly tail to warn other beavers in the area that a predator is approaching.

There were once more than 60 million beavers in North America. However, due to hunting for its _____ and glands for medicine, as well as the beavers' tree-felling and damming affecting other land uses, the population has declined to around 12 million.

Beavers can live in the _____ for up to 24 years.

Extra Credit: Answer These 3 questions:

1. Are beavers friendly?

2. Why are beavers' teeth orange?

3. How many beavers live in a dam?

3rd Grade Science: Helium

One of the lightest elements in the universe, helium is also one of its most common. In the periodic table, it is at the top of the noble gas group.

Helium is an odorless, tasteless, and colorless gas at room temperature. It has very low boiling and melting points, so it is usually found in the gas phase except in the most extreme conditions. Helium is the only element that does not solidify at normal pressures and remains a liquid even when temperatures reach absolute zero.

Helium is classified as an inert or noble gas. This means that the electrons in its outer electron shell are filled. As a result, it is highly inert and non-flammable.

Helium is a relatively rare element on Earth. It eventually escapes into space because it is so light; it is very little in the Earth's atmosphere.

Scientists believe that the majority of the helium in the universe was created during the universe's formation. However, new helium is produced in the cores of stars and through radioactive decay on Earth. Helium can be found trapped underground in natural gas reservoirs as a result of radioactive decay. The majority of the world's helium comes from gas deposits in the United States. Smaller quantities are available in Qatar, Algeria, Russia, Canada, China, and Poland.

The internal cores of stars are constantly producing helium. Intense pressures deep within a star cause hydrogen atoms to convert to helium atoms. This generates the energy, heat, and light required to power the stars and the sun. This process is known as nuclear fusion.

Helium is used to make balloons and airships float. Although it is not as light as hydrogen, it is a safer gas because hydrogen is highly flammable. Underwater, deep-sea divers breathe a mixture of helium and oxygen. Helium protects divers from being poisoned by too much oxygen. However, inhaling too much helium is also dangerous. The body may not receive enough oxygen, causing the person to suffocate.

MRI scanners, which use the gas to keep superconducting magnets cool, are the largest industrial users of helium gas. Other applications include silicon wafers for electronics and arc welding protection gas.

Astronomer Pierre Janssen discovered helium for the first time in 1868. When he was studying a solar eclipse, he found a new element. The element was discovered on Earth for the first time in 1895.

Helium derives its name from the Greek word "helios," which means "sun." Helios is also the name of the Greek Sun God.

Helium has eight different isotopes. Helium-4 is the most abundant of the helium isotopes, and it was largely created at the beginning of the universe.

1. **Helium is an ___, ___, and colorless gas at room temperature.**
   a. orderly, tasteful
   b. odorless, tasteless

2. **Helium is one of the _____ elements in the universe.**
   a. heaviest
   b. lightest

3. **Helium is classified as an inert or _____ gas.**
   a. noble
   b. odor

4. **_____Pierre Janssen discovered helium for the first time in 1868.**
   a. Scientist
   b. Astronomer

5. **Helium is used to make ____ and airships float.**

    a. kites

    b. balloons

6. **The internal cores of ____ are constantly producing helium.**

    a. stars

    b. the sun

7. **Helium protects divers from being poisoned by too much ____.**

    a. oxygen

    b. gas

8. **Helium can be found trapped underground in ____ gas reservoirs as a result of radioactive decay.**

    a. natural

    b. minerals

Extra Credit: Answer The Following 3 Questions:

1. What is helium made from?

2. Can you make a balloon float without helium?

3. Why did my helium balloons sink overnight?

_____

_____

_____

_____

_____

_____

_____

_____

_____

_____

_____

_____

3rd Grade Life Skills: Internet Safety

First, read the entire passage. After that, go back and fill in the blanks. You can skip the blanks you're unsure about and finish them later.

inappropriate	videos	unsupervised	downloading	violation
safety	skills	passwords	personal	permission
hurtful	protect	uncomfortable	agree	

Internet _____ is the act of making one's self safer while surfing the web. This includes being aware of the risks associated with your online activity and implementing a few solutions to minimize or eliminate these risks.

You may enjoy going online to watch _____, play games, and communicate with friends and family. You may be using the internet for schoolwork and homework as well. Computers, mobile phones, tablets, and other internet-enabled devices, including toys, can be used for this purpose.

Because you are becoming more independent online and may go online _____, you face more internet safety risks than younger children. There are additional dangers if you use the internet to communicate with others, such as on social media or in games.

You _____ yourself from potentially harmful or inappropriate content and activities when you take practical internet safety precautions. And you get to make the most of your online experience, which allows you to learn, explore, be creative, and connect with others.

10 Rules To Follow:

1. Unless my parents have given me permission, I will not give out _____ information such as my home address, phone number, or my parents' work address/phone number.

2. If I come across something that makes me _____, I will immediately notify my parents.

3. I will never _____ to meet someone I "met" online without first discussing with my parents. If my parents agree to the meeting, I will make sure that it is held in a public location and bring a parent with me.

4. If my parents think a picture of me or someone else online is _____, I will

discuss the issue with them and refrain from posting it.

5. I will not respond to any _____ messages or make me feel uncomfortable in any way. I don't believe that it is my fault if I receive such a message. If I do, I will immediately notify my parents.

6) I will talk to my parents about setting up rules for using the internet and mobile phones. We will work together to determine when I can be online, how long I can be online, and where I can go. Without their _____, I will not be able to access other areas or break these rules.

7. Other than my parents, I will not share my _____ with anyone else (even if they are my best friends).

8. I will consult with my parents before _____ or installing software or doing anything else that could potentially harm our computer or mobile device or that could compromise my family's privacy.

9. I will responsibly conduct myself on the internet, refraining from doing anything that is harmful to others or in _____ of the law.

10. I will educate my parents on how I have fun and learn new _____ online and teach them about the internet, computers, and other technology.

Extra Credit: Answer These 2 questions:

1. What is meant by Internet safety?

2. How can you stay safe on the Internet?

3rd Grade Science: The Moon Walk

On July 20, 1969, a record-breaking event occurred when millions of people gathered around their television sets to witness two American astronauts accomplish something no one had ever done before. Neil Armstrong and Edwin "Buzz" Aldrin became the first humans to walk on the moon, wearing bulky spacesuits and oxygen backpacks.

Armstrong famously said after the two stepped onto the lunar surface, "That's one small step for a man, one giant leap for mankind."

Russia launched the first artificial satellite, Sputnik 1, into space in 1957. Following that, the United States launched several satellites of its own. Both countries wanted to be the first to send a person into space.

It wasn't until 1961 that a person went into space: Russian Yuri Gagarin became the first on April 12, 1961. Alan Shepard of the United States became the first American in space less than a month later. Following these achievements, President John F. Kennedy challenged the National Aeronautics and Space Administration (NASA) to land a man on the moon in ten years or less.

NASA got right to work. On July 16, 1969, the Apollo 11 spacecraft was preparing to launch three astronauts into space.

As part of the selection process for the Apollo 11 astronauts, officials from NASA chose Neil Armstrong, Buzz Aldrin, and Michael Collins. The spacecraft approached the moon's surface just four days after taking off from Florida's Kennedy Space Center.

The three men separated before landing. Collins boarded Apollo 11's command module, the Columbia, from which he would remain in lunar orbit. Armstrong and Aldrin boarded the Eagle, Apollo 11's lunar module, and began their descent to the moon's surface.

The Eagle made a daring landing in a shallow moon crater known as the Sea of Tranquility, which was a risky move. Most people who watched the landing on television were unaware that the Eagle had only 20 seconds of landing fuel remaining at this point in the flight.

1. Neil _____ and Edwin "Buzz" ____ became the first humans to walk on the moon.
   a. Armstrong and Aldrin
   b. Armadale and Aladdin

2. Russia launched the first artificial satellite called ____.
   a. Spank 1.0
   b. Sputnik 1

3. The Eagle made a daring landing in a shallow moon crater known as the ____.
   a. Sea of Tranquility
   b. U.S.A Sea of Trinity

4. On ____, the Apollo 11 spacecraft was preparing to launch three astronauts into space.
   a. July 16, 1989
   b. July 16, 1969

5. Russian _____ became the first person in space on April 12, 1961
   a. Yuri Gagarin
   b. Yari Kim Jun

6. Armstrong and Aldrin boarded the ____, Apollo 11's lunar module, and began their descent to the moon's surface.
   a. Eagle
   b. Black Bird

3rd Grade Science: The First Moon Walk Part II

Looking out the windows, Armstrong and Aldrin saw a lifeless and barren lunar landscape from inside the spacecraft. In other words, the moon surface appeared dry, bare with no sign of life

The pair inside the Eagle prepared to exit the module after six and a half hours. Armstrong took the lead as mission commander and became the first person to set foot on the moon.

Aldrin descended the ladder and joined his partner twenty minutes later. Following a plaque reading that stated they "came in peace for all mankind," the two planted the American flag on the surface. President Richard Nixon called to express his congratulations to the astronauts.

Armstrong and Aldrin returned to their jobs, collecting moon rocks and dust samples for future research and development. After more than two hours, the astronauts re-boarded the lunar module and prepared to rejoin Collins. It was time to return home.

On July 24, 1969, the Apollo 11 crew returned to Earth. Ten astronauts would follow in Armstrong and Aldrin's footsteps over the next several years. The last moon mission took place in 1972.

Despite the fact that humans have not returned to the moon since then, they have continued to explore the cosmos. They even built the International Space Station (ISS), a space research station where they can conduct experiments and study space from a close distance.

NASA is currently working on sending humans to another planet: Mars. NASA is optimistic about its chances as a result of the Apollo 11 moon landing. The act of landing three people on the moon and safely returning them proved that successful human space exploration is possible.

1. **NASA is currently working on sending humans to another planet: ____.**
   a. Saturn
   b. Mars

2. **On ____, the Apollo 11 crew returned to Earth.**
   a. July 24, 1969
   b. July 25, 1967

3. **The _____ is a space research station.**
   a. US International Center Moon
   b. International Space Station

4. **Armstrong took the lead as mission _____ and became the first person to set foot on the moon.**
   a. commander
   b. scientist

5. **The astronauts saw a _____ reading that stated they "came in peace for all mankind,".**
   a. written letter
   b. plaque

6. **The last moon mission took place in _____.**
   a. 1972
   b. 1975

The Moon Walk Extra Credit: Answer The Following 3 Questions:

1. How old was Neil Armstrong when he landed on the moon?

2. Is the flag still on the moon?

3. What was the first animal in space?

3rd Grade Art Words

Art truly is a gift to the world. It is what we seek in our human experience. Art gives meaning to our lives and aids in our understanding of the world around us. It is an important part of our culture because it helps us understand our emotions better, increases our self-awareness, and allows us to be open to new ideas and experiences. As a result, art continues to open our minds and hearts and show us what is possible in our world. Art appreciation improves our quality of life and makes us feel good, according to scientific studies. We improve our problem-solving abilities and open our minds to new ideas when we create art.

Instructions: Match the Art words to the correct meaning.

#	Word		Meaning	
1	Contrast		A closed line.	A
2	Composition		The arrangement of forms in a work of art.	B
3	Cool colors		The area between and around objects.	C
4	Hue		Use of opposites near or beside one another (light and dark, rough and smooth)	D
5	Intensity		The dark values of a color (adding black).	E
6	Texture		Red, orange, yellow.	F
7	Subject matter		The center of interest of an artwork; the part you look at first.	G
8	Tint		Refers to the way things feel or look as though they might feel if they were touched.	H
9	Shade		The topic of interest or the primary theme of an artwork.	I
10	Warm colors		Principle of design concerned with difference or contrast.	J
11	Variety		Brightness of a color.	K
12	Focal point		Light values of a color (adding white)	L
13	Line		The surface quality that can be seen and felt.	M
14	Shape		Mostly green, blue, violet (purple).	N
15	Space		A mark with greater length than width.	O
16	Texture		The name of a color – red blue, yellow, etc.	P

Extra Credit Question: What are the elements of art? List each of them with a description.

3rd Grade Music: The Orchestra Vocabulary Words

Name: _____

Date: _____

Who wants to attend an orchestral performance? Obviously, you do! Orchestras are fantastic. An orchestra, at its most basic, is a large musical ensemble. Traditional orchestras have sections for woodwind, brass, strings, and percussion instruments.

The orchestra as we know it today originated in the early 1600s. Instruments were added and removed over the next several centuries, and what we now call the modern orchestra began to take shape. Violins became the orchestra's primary string instrument in the 17th century. More woodwind instruments were added over time, and by the 18th century, French horns, trombones, and trumpets were commonplace.

Throughout the 17th century, orchestras were small, with only about 18-20 members, and the composer was often a performer, often on the harpsichord or violin. As a result, there was no real director. In the 18th century, composers like Johann Sebastian Bach and Wolfgang Amadeus Mozart made orchestral music famous and influential, inspiring kings and peasants alike. During this period, concert performance indeed became a respected profession.

Ludwig van Beethoven, a 19th-century composer who standardized the orchestra using pairs of each woodwind and brass instrument, took the next big step. Beethoven composed works that made full use of the entire range of instruments, from high to low, and gave each section more critical roles, rather than letting the strings carry the majority of the melody on their own.

_____

Unscramble the names of the instruments found in the orchestra.

woodwind	cello	xylophone	violin	piano	trumpet
drums	oboe	brass	trombone	flute	clarinet
percussion	conductor	saxophone	harp		

1. tulef   _ _ _ t _

2. involi   v _ _ _ i _

3. eoob   _ _ _ e

4. articlne   _ _ _ _ i n _ _

5. srudm   d _ _ _ _

6. ddnwoiwo   w _ _ d _ _ _ _

7. rbass   b _ _ _ _

8. uniocrspse _ e _ c _ _ _ _ _ n

9. lceol   _ _ _ _ o

10. ahrp   _ _ _ p

11. erpttum   _ _ u _ _ e _

12. rootmebn   _ _ o m _ _ _ _

13. enlhoxypo   _ _ l _ _ _ _ _ e

14. udcootrnc   c _ _ _ u _ _ _ _

15. oniap   _ _ _ n _

16. heonoasxp   _ _ x _ _ _ o _ _

Cursive Writing Practice

Why did the teacher wear

sunglasses? (Because her

students were bright!) Why

was the teacher cross-eyed?

(She couldn't control her

pupils!) How do bees get to

school? (By school buzz!)

What did the paper say to

the pencil? (Write on!) How

do you get straight As? (Use

Cursive Writing Practice

Score: _____   Date: _____

a ruler!) What building has

the most stories? (The

library!) What do you get

when you throw a million

books into the ocean? (A

title wave!) What is snake's

favorite subject? (Hiss-tory!)

Why did the teacher write on

the window? (To make the

lesson very clear!)

EASTER CROSSWORD

Easter, also known as Resurrection Day, is an annual spring holiday. It is a Christian celebration of Jesus Christ's resurrection from the dead. It is considered the most important day of the year by Christians. Non-Christians may observe Easter as the start of the spring season. Even if they do not regularly attend church, many people attend an Easter service.

Every year, Easter is not celebrated on the same day. This is known as a moveable feast. Currently, all Christian churches agree on how to calculate the date. Easter is observed on the first Sunday following the first full moon after March 21st. This means it takes place in March or April. It could happen as early as March 22 or as late as April 25.

KIDS crossword

"Happy Easter day"

D	A	X	Q	P	C	X	E	C	L
T	P	T	V	J	H	C	F	A	S
V	R	T	U	L	I	P	S	R	T
L	I	M	A	A	C	Z	U	R	V
Q	L	A	M	B	K	S	B	O	B
Y	C	H	O	C	O	L	A	T	E
L	Y	G	R	A	S	S	S	L	G
C	W	B	E	A	N	S	K	R	G
D	M	N	D	H	R	H	E	S	S
R	L	Q	Q	H	U	N	T	M	N

BASKET
CHICK
CHOCOLATE
HUNT
CARROT
LAMB
EGGS
BEANS
TULIPS
APRIL
GRASS

HEALTHY GREENS CROSSWORD

Humans have consumed leafy greens since prehistoric times. However, it wasn't until the first Africans arrived in North America in the early 1600s that the continent got its first real taste of dark green leafy vegetables, which they grew for themselves and their families. Cooked greens evolved into a traditional African American food over time. They eventually became essential in Southern regional diets and are now enjoyed across the country.

Dark green leafy vegetables are high in nutrients. Salad greens, kale, and spinach are high in vitamins A, C, E, and K, while broccoli, bok choy, and mustard are high in various B vitamins. These vegetables are also high in carotenoids, which are antioxidants that protect cells and help to prevent cancer in its early stages. They are also high in fiber, iron, magnesium, potassium, and calcium. Greens also have a low carbohydrate, sodium, and cholesterol content.

KIDS crossword

"Healthy greens"

U	V	B	E	A	N	S	N	T	F	J
O	I	A	V	O	C	A	D	O	M	T
W	N	Z	U	C	C	H	I	N	I	F
Q	P	N	C	U	C	U	M	B	E	R
E	F	E	C	A	B	B	A	G	E	Z
C	A	U	L	I	F	L	O	W	E	R
P	E	V	S	Q	U	A	S	H	A	D
E	B	A	R	T	I	C	H	O	K	E
A	G	B	R	O	C	C	O	L	I	Y
S	P	R	O	U	T	S	F	P	N	B
U	Z	A	S	P	A	R	A	G	U	S

ARTICHOKE
SQUASH
BROCCOLI
CAULIFLOWER
CUCUMBER
CABBAGE
ASPARAGUS
AVOCADO
ZUCCHINI
BEANS
PEAS
SPROUTS

Brain Teaser: Spot the Difference

1. You have to remember what you see in one picture and compare it to what you see in the other picture
2. You have to mark or circle the locations where you see a difference

Ready! Set! Go!

Brain Teaser: Spot the Difference

1. You have to remember what you see in one picture and compare it to what you see in the other picture
2. You have to mark or circle the locations where you see a difference

Ready! Set! Go!

FIND
6
DIFFERENCES

Brain Teaser: Spot the Difference

1. You have to remember what you see in one picture and compare it to what you see in the other picture
2. You have to mark or circle the locations where you see a difference

Ready! Set! Go!

Brain Teaser: Spot the Difference

1. You have to remember what you see in one picture and compare it to what you see in the other picture
2. You have to mark or circle the locations where you see a difference

Ready! Set! Go!

3rd Grade Art: Draw Facial Expressions

Facial expressions are one of the most effective ways for humans to communicate with one another. We learn to distinguish between a happy and an angry expression from a very young age. As we get older, we develop the ability to express our feelings and read other people's thoughts and emotions without using words.

Try looking at photos of yourself or others expressing various emotions and studying them to identify which parts of your face are moving. It is a great way to start learning how to draw facial expressions and understand points of tension. The more intense the emotion, the more areas of the face are involved.

3rd Grade Art: Finish
The Pictures & Color

Finish the picture

	a	b	c	d
1				
2				
3				
4				

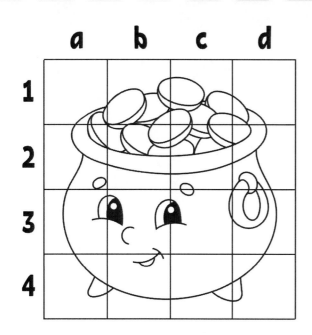

	a	b	c	d
1				
2				
3				
4				

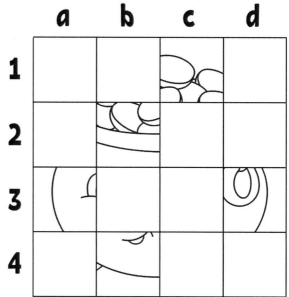

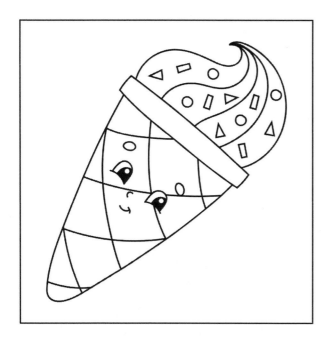

3rd Grade Life Skills: Making Friends

People find it difficult to believe, but I used to **walk** around school by myself.

I spent all of my energy attempting to **persuade** other students that I was interesting.

Being interested in others was the key to **opening** the door to making friends for me.

A smile may appear to be such a simple thing to do, but it can start a lot of **friendships** .

Now, I'm not suggesting that you walk around with a **grin** on your face all day because people will think you're weird.

Everyone wishes to be heard. It's easy to believe that the best way to make friends is to **brag** about how cool you are.

Everyone wants to feel like they are the most **important** person in the room.

I used to **dream** about being so well-known that I didn't have time to do anything other than saying "hi" to people as I walked by.

You will have a much happier school life if you have a few good friends rather than a tight connection to the **entire** school. What you are interested in is reflected in your friends.

Knowing who you allow you to be yourself. Perhaps you enjoy watching silly stuff on YouTube, riding your **bike** , or cooking Tacos every Tuesday.

Extra Credit: Answer These 2 questions: 1. What are 3 ways to make friends? 2. What is the difference between acquaintance and friend?

[NO ANSWERS. INDEPENDENT RESEARCH]

Simple Fractions ANSWERS

1) $\dfrac{3}{11}$ + $\dfrac{4}{11}$ = $\dfrac{7}{11}$

2) $\dfrac{1}{10}$ + $\dfrac{6}{10}$ = $\dfrac{7}{10}$

3) $\dfrac{4}{11}$ + $\dfrac{5}{11}$ = $\dfrac{9}{11}$

4) $\dfrac{3}{12}$ + $\dfrac{6}{12}$ = $\dfrac{9}{12}$

5) $\dfrac{1}{4}$ + $\dfrac{2}{4}$ = $\dfrac{3}{4}$

ANSWERS
Adding Fractions

1) $\dfrac{5}{7} + \dfrac{4}{7} = \dfrac{5}{7} + \dfrac{4}{7} = \dfrac{9}{7} = 1\dfrac{2}{7}$

2) $\dfrac{2}{8} + \dfrac{5}{8} = \dfrac{2}{8} + \dfrac{5}{8} = \dfrac{7}{8}$

3) $\dfrac{6}{7} + \dfrac{4}{7} = \dfrac{6}{7} + \dfrac{4}{7} = \dfrac{10}{7} = 1\dfrac{3}{7}$

4) $\dfrac{5}{4} + \dfrac{3}{4} = \dfrac{5}{4} + \dfrac{3}{4} = \dfrac{8}{4} = \dfrac{2}{1} = 2\dfrac{0}{1}$

5) $\dfrac{1}{8} + \dfrac{3}{8} = \dfrac{1}{8} + \dfrac{3}{8} = \dfrac{4}{8} = \dfrac{1}{2}$

6) $\dfrac{2}{6} + \dfrac{5}{6} = \dfrac{2}{6} + \dfrac{5}{6} = \dfrac{7}{6} = 1\dfrac{1}{6}$

7) $\dfrac{2}{6} + \dfrac{2}{6} = \dfrac{2}{6} + \dfrac{2}{6} = \dfrac{4}{6} = \dfrac{2}{3}$

8) $\dfrac{5}{4} + \dfrac{3}{4} = \dfrac{5}{4} + \dfrac{3}{4} = \dfrac{8}{4} = \dfrac{2}{1} = 2\dfrac{0}{1}$

9) $\dfrac{8}{8} + \dfrac{6}{8} = \dfrac{8}{8} + \dfrac{6}{8} = \dfrac{14}{8} = \dfrac{7}{4} = 1\dfrac{3}{4}$

10) $\dfrac{3}{7} + \dfrac{5}{7} = \dfrac{3}{7} + \dfrac{5}{7} = \dfrac{8}{7} = 1\dfrac{1}{7}$

11) $\dfrac{7}{9} + \dfrac{1}{9} = \dfrac{7}{9} + \dfrac{1}{9} = \dfrac{8}{9}$

12) $\dfrac{3}{9} + \dfrac{6}{9} = \dfrac{3}{9} + \dfrac{6}{9} = \dfrac{9}{9} = 1$

13) $\dfrac{2}{7} + \dfrac{4}{7} = \dfrac{2}{7} + \dfrac{4}{7} = \dfrac{6}{7}$

14) $\dfrac{3}{6} + \dfrac{2}{6} = \dfrac{3}{6} + \dfrac{2}{6} = \dfrac{5}{6}$

15) $\dfrac{3}{6} + \dfrac{5}{6} = \dfrac{3}{6} + \dfrac{5}{6} = \dfrac{8}{6} = \dfrac{4}{3} = 1\dfrac{1}{3}$

Greatest Common Factor ANSWERS

1)   15 , 3   3

2)   24 , 12   12

3)   10 , 4   2

4)   40 , 4   4

5)   8 , 40   8

6)   10 , 4   2

7)   12 , 20   4

8)   5 , 20   5

9)   8 , 2   2

10)   24 , 40   8

11)   6 , 8   2

12)   10 , 3   1

13)   8 , 6   2

14)   24 , 10   2

15)   24 , 12   12

16)   40 , 24   8

17)   8 , 10   2

18)   10 , 20   10

19)   2 , 3   1

20)   6 , 12   6

Prime Factors ANSWERS

1) 38   2 , 19

2) 49   7

3) 35   5 , 7

4) 25   5

5) 15   3 , 5

6) 44   2 , 11

7) 32   2

8) 48   2 , 3

9) 22   2 , 11

10) 21   3 , 7

11) 30   2 , 3 , 5

12) 20   2 , 5

13) 39   3 , 13

14) 14   2 , 7

15) 12   2 , 3

16) 26   2 , 13

17) 46   2 , 23

18) 40   2 , 5

19) 24   2 , 3

20) 10   2 , 5

ANSWERS

Find the Prime Factors of the Numbers

1)

```
        ┌────┐
        │ 27 │
        └────┘
        ╱    ╲
      (3)   ┌───┐
            │ 9 │
            └───┘
            ╱   ╲
          (3)   (3)
```

Factors

3 x 3 x 3 = 27

2)

```
        ┌────┐
        │ 52 │
        └────┘
        ╱    ╲
      (2)   ┌────┐
            │ 26 │
            └────┘
            ╱    ╲
          (2)   (13)
```

Factors

2 x 2 x 13 = 52

3)

```
        ┌────┐
        │ 44 │
        └────┘
        ╱    ╲
      (2)   ┌────┐
            │ 22 │
            └────┘
            ╱    ╲
          (2)   (11)
```

Factors

2 x 2 x 11 = 44

---

4)

```
        ┌────┐
        │ 30 │
        └────┘
        ╱    ╲
      (2)   ┌────┐
            │ 15 │
            └────┘
            ╱    ╲
          (3)   (5)
```

Factors

2 x 3 x 5 = 30

5)

```
        ┌────┐
        │ 24 │
        └────┘
        ╱    ╲
      (2)   ┌────┐
            │ 12 │
            └────┘
            ╱    ╲
         ┌───┐  (2)
         │ 6 │
         └───┘
         ╱   ╲
       (2)   (3)
```

Factors

2 x 2 x 2 x 3 = 24

6)

```
        ┌────┐
        │ 28 │
        └────┘
        ╱    ╲
      (2)   ┌────┐
            │ 14 │
            └────┘
            ╱    ╲
          (2)   (7)
```

Factors

2 x 2 x 7 = 28

ANSWERS
Rearranging Digits

1) 399   993

2) 744   744

3) 488   884

4) 616   661

5) 734   743

6) 846   864

7) 844   844

8) 345   543

9) 959   995

10) 559   955

1) 897   789

2) 696   669

3) 825   258

4) 135   135

5) 751   157

6) 149   149

7) 862   268

8) 212   122

9) 557   557

10) 675   567

ANSWERS
Rearranging Digits

1) 1,182   8,211   6) 7,769   9,776

2) 1,549   9,541   7) 7,521   7,521

3) 5,366   6,653   8) 8,146   8,641

4) 3,869   9,863   9) 8,161   8,611

5) 2,853   8,532   10) 7,769   9,776

1) 7,816   1,678   6) 6,636   3,666

2) 3,827   2,378   7) 8,176   1,678

3) 4,946   4,469   8) 9,222   2,229

4) 5,938   3,589   9) 2,172   1,227

5) 1,627   1,267   10) 5,366   3,566

TIME ANSWERS

What time is on the clock?   6:00

What time was it 1 hour ago?   5:00

What time was it 3 hours and 40 minutes ago?   2:20

What time will it be in 4 hours and 20 minutes?   10:20

What time is on the clock?   7:40

What time was it 2 hours ago?   5:40

What time will it be in 3 hours ?   10:40

What time will it be in 4 hours and 20 minutes?   12:00

What time is on the clock?   10:20

What time was it 1 hour ago?   9:20

What time was it 3 hours and 20 minutes ago?   7:00

What time will it be in 2 hours ?   12:20

What time is on the clock?   10:00

What time will it be in 3 hours and 20 minutes?   1:20

What time was it 2 hours ago?   8:00

What time was it 1 hour ago?   9:00

3rd Grade Grammar:
Homophones vs Homographs
vs. Homonyms

1. 'there,' 'their,' or 'they're' are examples of _____.

    a. Homophones

    b. Homographs

2. ____ are words that have the same spelling or pronunciation but different meanings.

    a. Homonyms

    b. Hemograms

3. Choose the correct homophone for this sentence: Please don't drop and _____that bottle of hand sanitizer!

    a. brake

    b. break

4. Homographs are two or more words that have the same spelling but different ____.

    a. ending sounds

    b. meanings

5. Current (A flow of water / Up to date) is both homograph and homophone.

    a. True

    b. False

6. To, two and too are _____.

    a. Homonyms

    b. Homagraphs

7. The candle filled the _____ with a delicious scent.

    a. air

    b. heir

8. Kim drove _____ the tunnel.

    a. threw

    b. through

9. John wants to go to _____ house for dinner, but they don't like her, so _____ going to say no.

    a. there, they're

    b. their, they're

10. We won a $95,000 _____!

    a. check

    b. cheque

11. For example, a pencil is not really made with _____.

    a. led

    b. lead

12. Choose the correct homophone for this sentence: Timmy was standing _____ in line.

    a. fourth

    b. forth

13. Homophones are two words that sound the same but have a different meaning.

    a. True

    b. False

14. The word ring in the following two sentences is considered what? She wore a ruby ring. | We heard the doorbell ring.

    a. hologram

    b. homograph

15. A Homograph is a word that has more than one meaning and doesn't have to sound the same.

    a. True

    b. False

16. Homophones occur when there are multiple ways to spell the same sound.

    a. True

    b. False

17. Select the correct homophone: I have very little (patience/patients) when students do not follow directions.
    a. patience
    b. patients

18. The correct homophone (s) are used in the sentence: Personally, I hate the smell of read meet.
    a. True
    b. False

19. The correct homophone(s) is used in the sentence: We saw a herd of cattle in the farmer's field.
    a. True
    b. False

20. What is NOT an example of a homograph?
    a. or, oar
    b. live, live

21. I love my _____ class.
    a. dear
    b. deer

22. We will go _____ after we finish our lesson.
    a. there
    b. their

23. Please grab _____ jacket for recess.
    a. you're
    b. your

24. There is _____ more water at the concession stand.
    a. no
    b. know

Grammar: Personal Pronouns

1. Pronouns stand-in for the people and ____.
   - a. animals
   - b. nothing at all

2. Using pronouns allows a speaker or writer to vary how they refer to a ____.
   - a. adverb
   - b. noun

3. The tie is very special. ___ is a magic tie.
   - a. He
   - b. It

4. Charlie and I went to a pond. _____ saw two frogs.
   - a. They
   - b. We

5. The turtle is tired. _____ is rest under the tree.
   - a. Him
   - b. It

6. Tim and I saw the lion in the jungle. ____ were very afraid.
   - a. Their
   - b. We

7. The rabbit escaped from the trap and ran away. _____ was safe.
   - a. They
   - b. It

8. The farmer's wife saw a wolf. _____ shouted to the farmer for help.
   - a. She
   - b. It

9. The boys found a magic chain. _____ gave it to the queen.
   - a. They
   - b. He

10. _____ 20 years old.
    - a. Them
    - b. She's

11. _____ house is big.
    - a. He
    - b. His

12. _____ name's Farah.
    - a. Her
    - b. She

13. How old is she?
    - a. He's seven.
    - b. She's seven.

14. What's his name?
    - a. His name's Ali.
    - b. Her name's Ali.

15. Mia and Omar enjoy listening to Ree's singing. Becomes:
    - a. Them enjoy listening to Ree's singing.
    - b. They enjoy listening to Ree's singing.

16. Dana kicked the ball. Becomes:
    - a. She kicked the ball.
    - b. He kicked the ball.

17. The dog is barking. _____ is barking at someone.
    - a. He
    - b. It

18. My sister likes basketball. _____ plays everyday.
    - a. She
    - b. He

3rd Grade Grammar: Contractions

Take a moment to visualize the process of blowing up a balloon. It grows larger and larger. When we let the air out, it shrinks or contracts. To contract means to shrink, reduce or get smaller.

In writing, a contraction is a word that combines two words to form a shorter word. In other words, the contraction makes the two words smaller. A contraction is simply a word that is a shortened form of two words combined.

When the words can and not are combined, the contraction word can't is formed. The apostrophe (as in this symbol: ') is a small punctuation mark that replaces the letters that have been removed. The apostrophe replaces the 'n' and the 'o' of not in can't.

	A	B	C	D
1.	**he'd**	ha'd	hh'd	hp'd
2.	yoo'rre	yoo're	you'rre	**you're**
3.	wesn't	wassn't	wascn't	**wasn't**
4.	sied	mhod	sha'd	**she'd**
5.	**they'll**	thay'l	they'l	thay'll
6.	aran't	arran't	**aren't**	arren't
7.	**let's**	latt's	lett's	lat's
8.	lad	I's	**I'd**	wts
9.	she'l	sha'l	**she'll**	sha'll
10.	wa'e	wa've	wa'va	**we've**
11.	yoo'd	yood	yuo'd	**you'd**
12.	ha'l	ha'll	he'l	**he'll**
13.	**I've**	I'vw	Ikva	I'va
14.	hesn't	hassn't	hascn't	**hasn't**
15.	thai'd	thay'd	**they'd**	thei'd
16.	**you'll**	yoo'll	you'l	yoo'l
17.	haven'tt	havan't	**haven't**	havan'tt
18.	wa'll	we'l	wa'l	**we'll**
19.	yoo've	yoo'e	yuo've	**you've**
20.	**hadn't**	hedn't	hedn'tt	hadn'tt
21.	havan'tt	haven'tt	**haven't**	havan't

3rd Grade Grammar:
Contractions Sentence Building

Contracted words, also known as contractions, are short words formed by combining two words. In the contraction, letters are omitted and replaced with an apostrophe. The apostrophe indicates where the letters would be if the words were written in its entirety.

Practice *sentence* building. *Unscramble* the words to form a complete sentence and CIRCLE the contraction in each sentence.

1. Who's coming to your party? _____

    your · Who's

2. He's not coming with us. _____

    with · coming

3. Aren't you Caroline's friend? _____

    you · Caroline's

4. I wouldn't go in there if I were you. _____

    you. · I · go · I

5. I'm ready for a vacation. _____

    I'm · a

6. He's going to Florida for the holiday. _____

    Florida · going · holiday.

7. We're staying in town. _____

    We're · town.

8. They're undecided at the moment. _____

    They're · undecided

9. I'll see you next week. _____

    I'll · week.

10. I'm going for a walk. _____

    I'm · a

11. It's freezing outside!

outside!

12. I can't find my glasses anywhere.

I   find   can't

13. I shouldn't have eaten so much!

so   shouldn't   eaten

14. What's the time?

What's

15. Where's my newspaper?

my

16. When's your wedding?

When's

17. Let's go to the store.

the   store.

18. I'm ready to go now.

go   to

19. You're welcome to come along.

welcome   to

20. I've been to the store already.

store   the   been

21. He isn't planning to come along.

along.   to   come

22. She hasn't made up her mind yet.

mind   up   She

3rd Grade Grammar:
SUPERLATIVE ADJECTIVES

A superlative adjective is a comparative adjective that describes something as being of the highest degree or extreme. When comparing three or more people or things, we use superlative adjectives. Superlative adjectives typically end in 'est'. Examples of superlative adjectives include the words biggest and fastest.

Unscramble Word Tip: Try solving the easy words first, and then go back and answer the more difficult ones.

prettiest	hottest	crowded	friendliest	biggest	smallest
saddest	best	worst	tallest	shortest	longest
fattest	newest	heaviest	nicest	beautiful	expensive
cheapest	comfortable	youngest	largest		

1. peehtsac   c h e a p e s t

2. talresg   l a r g e s t

3. ntogels   l o n g e s t

4. wsenet   n e w e s t

5. icetns   n i c e s t

6. tstosreh   s h o r t e s t

7. samlsetl   s m a l l e s t

8. lstteal   t a l l e s t

9. goysunte   y o u n g e s t

10. tggsbie   b i g g e s t

11. eftastt   f a t t e s t

12. ttoesht   h o t t e s t

13. adstdes   s a d d e s t

14. filtaubeu   b e a u t i f u l

15. ctlefarbmoo   c o m f o r t a b l e

16. ddrwoce   c r o w d e d

17. enpsvxeei   e x p e n s i v e

18. esdeirfiltn   f r i e n d l i e s t

19. hitvseea   h e a v i e s t

20. espttriet   p r e t t i e s t

21. bets   b e s t

22. wrsot   w o r s t

3rd Grade History: Thomas Edison

Thomas Alva Edison was born in Milan, Ohio, on February 11, 1847. He developed **hearing** loss at a young age. He was a creative and inquisitive child. However, he struggled in school, possibly because he couldn't hear his **teacher** . He was then educated at home by his mother.

Because of his numerous important inventions, Thomas Edison was nicknamed the "wizard." On his own or in collaboration with others, he has designed and built more than 1,000 **devices** . The phonograph (record player), the lightbulb, and the motion-picture projector are among his most notable inventions.

Although Thomas did not invent the first electric **light** bulb, he did create the first practical electric light bulb that could be manufactured and used in the home. He also **invented** other items required to make the light bulb usable in homes, such as safety fuses and on/off switches for light sockets.

As a teenager, Thomas worked as a telegraph operator. Telegraphy was one of the most important communication systems in the country at the time. Thomas was skilled at sending and receiving **Morse** code messages. He enjoyed tweaking with telegraphic instruments, and he came up with several improvements to make them even better. By early 1869, he had left his telegraphy job to pursue his **dream** of becoming a full-time inventor.

Edison worked tirelessly with scientists and other collaborators to complete projects. He established **research** facilities in Menlo Park, California, and West Orange, New Jersey. Finally, Edison established companies that manufactured and sold his successful inventions.

Edison's family was essential to him, even though he spent the majority of his life **dedicated** to his work. He had six children from two marriages. Edison **passed** away on October 18, 1931.

3rd Grade History: Christopher Columbus

	A	B	C	D
1.	**America**	Amerryca	Ameryca	Amerrica
2.	**spices**	spicesc	spises	spicess
3.	Eurropaen	**European**	Europaen	Eurropean
4.	**coast**	coasct	cuast	coasst
5.	abrroad	abruad	**abroad**	abrruad
6.	**sailor**	siallor	saillor	sialor
7.	**nations**	nattions	nascons	natsions
8.	explurers	**explorers**	expllorers	expllurers
9.	sylver	syllver	sillver	**silver**
10.	Spayn	Spian	Spyan	**Spain**
11.	Indains	Indainss	Indianss	**Indians**
12.	**discover**	disssover	disscover	dissover
13.	islend	iscland	**island**	issland

3rd Grade History Reading Comprehension: Walt Disney

On December 5, 1901, Walter Elias Disney was born in __Chicago__, Illinois. His family relocated to a farm outside of Marceline, Missouri, when he was __four__ years old, thanks to his parents, Elias and Flora. Walt loved growing up on the farm with his three older brothers (Herbert, Raymond, and Roy) and younger __sister__ (Ruth). Walt discovered his passion for drawing and art in Marceline.

The Disneys relocated to Kansas City after four years in Marceline. On weekends, Walt continued to draw and attend __art__ classes. He even bartered his drawings for free haircuts with a local barber. Walt got a summer job on a train. On the __train__, he walked back and forth, selling __snacks__ and newspapers. Walt had a great time on the train and would be fascinated by trains for the rest of his life.

Walt's family relocated to Chicago around the time he started high school. Walt studied at the Chicago Art Institute and worked as a cartoonist for the school __newspaper__. Walt decided at the age of sixteen that he wanted to fight in World War I. Due to the fact that he was still too young to join the army, he decided to drop out of school and join the __Red__ Cross instead.

Walt aspired to create his own animated cartoons. He founded his own company, Laugh-O-Gram. He sought the help of some of his __friends__, including Ubbe Iwerks.

Disney, on the other hand, was not going to be deterred by a single setback. In 1923, he relocated to __Hollywood__, California, and founded the Disney Brothers' Studio with his __brother__ Roy. He enlisted the services of Ubbe Iwerks and a number of other animators once more.

Walt had to start all over again. This time, he came up with a new character called __Mickey__ Mouse. The movie was a huge success. Disney kept working, creating new characters like __Donald__ Duck, Goofy, and Pluto.

In 1932, Walt Disney decided to create a full-length animated film called Snow __White__.

Disney used the proceeds from Snow White to establish a film studio and produce other animated films such as Pinocchio, Fantasia, Dumbo, Bambi, __Alice__ in Wonderland, and __Peter__ Pan.

Disney's Wonderful World of Color, the Davy Crockett series, and the Mickey Mouse __Club__ was among the first Disney television shows to air on network television.

Disney, who is constantly coming up with new ideas, had the idea to build a __theme__ park featuring rides and entertainment based on his films. In 1955, Disneyland opened its doors. It cost $17 million to construct. Although it wasn't an immediate success, Disney World has since grown into one of the world's most popular __vacation__ destinations.

Every year, millions of people enjoy his films and theme parks. Every year, his company continues to produce fantastic films and __entertainment__.

3rd Grade Reading
Comprehension Multiple Choice:
Walt Disney

Make sure you go back and read the Disney article through to the very end. If you attempt to complete this assignment solely by scanning for answers, you will almost certainly pick the incorrect answer. Take your time. Ask questions. Get help if you need it. Good Luck!

1. Walter Elias Disney was born in Chicago, ____.
   a. Illinois
   b. Italy

2. Walter's parents names were Elias and Flora.
   a. True
   b. False

3. Walt got a summer job on a _____.
   a. train
   b. boat

4. Walt's younger sister name was ____.
   a. Ruby
   b. Ruth

5. Walt had _____ brothers.
   a. three
   b. two

6. In 1923, walt relocated to Hollywood, _____.
   a. Colorado
   b. California

7. Steamboat ____ was the title of the film, which starred Mickey and Minnie Mouse.
   a. William
   b. Willie

8. Walt spent the next year in France driving _____ for the Red Cross.
   a. taxi cabs
   b. ambulances

9. Walt and his friends created the well-known character Oswald the Lucky _____t.
   a. Dog
   b. Rabbi

10. Walt's first color animated film was____.
    a. Bears and Tigers
    b. Flowers and Trees

11. In ____, Disneyland opened its doors.
    a. 1955
    b. 1995

12. _____ was among the first Disney television shows to air on network television.
    a. Mickey Mouse Club
    b. Mickey and Friends

13. _____ was his first major live-action film.
    a. Treasure Island
    b. Treats Island

14. Walt Disney decided to create a full-length animated film called _____.
    a. Snow White
    b. Robin Hood

Calendar Words Unscramble

Unscramble the days and months below.

August	November	Monday	May	April	June
Friday	March	January	September	October	July
Saturday	February	December	Sunday	Thursday	Tuesday
Wednesday					

1. nuayraj   J a n u a r y

2. beyuarrf   F e b r u a r y

3. mrach   M a r c h

4. arilp   A p r i l

5. amy   M a y

6. njeu   J u n e

7. yjlu   J u l y

8. uasutg   A u g u s t

9. beermstpe   S e p t e m b e r

10. borotec   O c t o b e r

11. rmnbeveo   N o v e m b e r

12. edebemrc   D e c e m b e r

13. oymdna   M o n d a y

14. styaued   T u e s d a y

15. ydsaeedwn W e d n e s d a y

16. hrtydasu   T h u r s d a y

17. dfiray   F r i d a y

18. srtduaay   S a t u r d a y

19. saduny   S u n d a y

3rd Grade Health Spelling
Words: Healthy Routines

Write the correct word for each sentence.

Reading	overeat	Eating	read	fat
fresh	fruit	health	glass	chair
floss	Breakfast	Staying	daily	Sleep
fiber	enough	burn	Walking	body

1. Creating a healthy __daily__ routine is simple.

2. __Staying__ hydrated is vital for our health.

3. Exercise has tremendous __health__ benefits.

4. Exposure to the sun enables the __body__ to produce vitamin D.

5. __Walking__ is one of the most underrated healthy habits you can do.

6. Vegetables are low in calories, yet high in vitamins, minerals, and __fiber__ .

7. __Reading__ has benefits to both your physical and mental health.

8. __Sleep__ is the only time during the day where our bodies are able to relax, unwind and recover.

9. __Eating__ a variety of good foods.

10. __Breakfast__ is the most important meal of the day.

11. Drink a __glass__ of water.

12. Sitting in your __chair__ all day long isn't good for you.

13. Excess body __fat__ comes from eating more than we need.

14. Cooking the right amount makes it easier to not __overeat__ .

15. Physical activity helps us __burn__ off the extra calories.

16. Eat __fruit__ instead of eating a candy bar.

17. Make time to __read__ every day.

18. Don't forget to __floss__ .

19. Swap sugary desserts for __fresh__ fruit.

20. Get __enough__ sleep.

3rd Grade Spelling Words
Unscramble

Unscramble Word Tip: Try solving the easy words first, and then go back and answer the more difficult ones.

compare	group	pond	taught	laundry	start
grade	wrap	front	stone	pardon	city
shirt	open	am	value	office	hope
highest	close	person	verb	hear	near
travel	pencil				

1. lseoc   c l o s e

2. oesnpr   p e r s o n

3. npdrao   p a r d o n

4. ma   a m

5. ntoes   s t o n e

6. earn   n e a r

7. ithrs   s h i r t

8. auevl   v a l u e

9. atelvr   t r a v e l

10. poeh   h o p e

11. tciy   c i t y

12. bvre   v e r b

13. aehr   h e a r

14. ndpo   p o n d

15. tuahgt   t a u g h t

16. adrge   g r a d e

17. ofrnt   f r o n t

18. trats   s t a r t

19. nydrual   l a u n d r y

20. enpo   o p e n

21. wapr   w r a p

22. ilencp   p e n c i l

23. gishteh   h i g h e s t

24. aempcro   c o m p a r e

25. orugp   g r o u p

26. oeffic   o f f i c e

3rd Grade Spelling Words
Crossword

Complete the crossword by filling in a word that fits each clue. Fill in the correct answers, one letter per square, both across and down, from the given clues. There will be a gray space between multi-word answers.

Tip: Solve the easy clues first, and then go back and answer the more difficult ones.

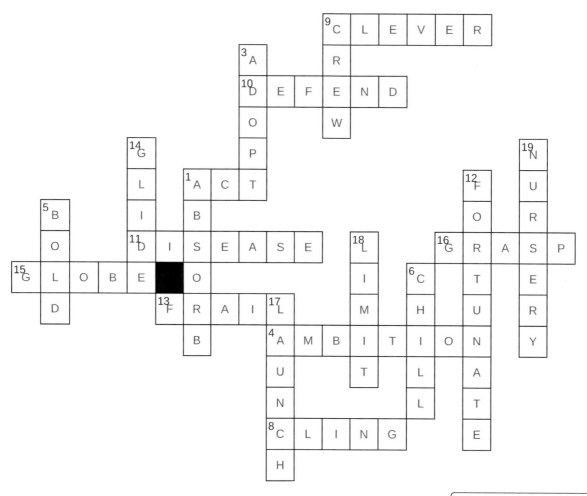

Across

1. behave in a certain manner
4. a strong drive for success
8. hold on tightly
9. mentally quick and resourceful
10. protect against a challenge or attack
11. an impairment of health
13. physically weak
15. an object with a spherical shape
16. hold firmly

Down

1. take in a liquid
3. take into one's family
5. fearless and daring
6. coldness due to a cold environment
9. an organized group of workers
12. having unexpected good luck
14. move smoothly and effortlessly
17. propel with force
18. as far as something can go
19. a child's room for a baby

ABSORB   ADOPT   DISEASE
LIMIT   ACT   CLEVER
AMBITION   NURSERY   FRAIL
BOLD   DEFEND   CHILL
GLIDE   GRASP   FORTUNATE
GLOBE   LAUNCH   CREW
CLING

3rd Grade Science Spelling Words

Instructions: Match the science words to the correct meaning.

1	C	Shadow	→	A dark area
2	K	Nectar	→	Juicy fluid within flowers
3	O	Prey	→	Kill and hunt for food
4	L	Gas	→	State of matter that can expand freely
5	G	Mixture	→	A combination of different things
6	M	Fossil	→	The remains of plant or animal
7	D	Bacteria	→	Unicellular microorganism
8	F	Brain	→	A coordinating organ of the human body
9	B	Geology	→	Study of earth
10	J	Atom	→	The smallest particle
11	A	Magnetic	→	Having magnetic properties
12	R	Dissolve	→	Solid form in any liquid
13	E	Fact	→	Any true information
14	I	Biology	→	The study of living beings
15	Q	Organism	→	An individual/living being
16	N	Scale	→	Bony plates in the fish skin
17	H	Test tube	→	A thin tube made up of glass
18	P	Weigh	→	Expression of heaviness

3rd Grade Storytime: Let Thy Hair Down

Once upon a time, there was a man and a woman who had long wished for a __child__ in desperation. Finally, the woman hoped that God was about to grant her wish.

These people had a __small__ window in the back of their house to see a beautiful garden.

One day, the woman was standing by this window, looking down into the garden, when she noticed a bed planted with the most beautiful rampion (rapunzel), and it looked so __fresh__ and green that she wanted so badly for it and sought to eat some.

This desire grew __stronger__ by the day, and because she knew she couldn't get any of it, she looked pale and miserable.

"Rather than letting your wife die, bring her some of the rampions yourself; let it cost you what it will!" thought the man who __loved__ her.

In the late afternoon, he __climbed__ over the wall into the Witch's garden, grabbed a handful of rampion, and hurriedly handed it to his wife.

But when he got down the wall, he was __terrified__ because he saw the Witch standing before him.

The Witch then softened her rage and said to him, "If the case is as you say, I will allow you to take as much rampion as you want, but there is one __condition__: you must give me the child that your wife will bring into the world." It will be well cared for, and I will look after it like a mother."

In his terror, the man __agreed__ to everything, and when the woman finally had a little daughter, the Witch appeared immediately, gave the child the name Rapunzel, and took it away with her.

When she was twelve years old, the Witch locked her in a __tower__ in the middle of a forest with no stairs or door.

3rd Grade Storytime: Let Thy Hair Down| Part 2

Rapunzel had magnificent __long__ hair as fine as spun gold, and when she heard the Witch's voice, she unfastened her long braided locks and wound them around one of the window hooks above.

After a year or two, the King's Son rode through the forest and passed by the __tower__ .

He rode home, but the singing had touched him so deeply that he went out into the __forest__ every day to listen to it.

When it got __dark__ the next day, he went to the tower and cried:

Rapunzel was __terrified__ at first when a man her eyes had never seen before approached her.

When he asked Rapunzel if she would take him as her __husband__ and she saw that he was young and handsome, she thought to herself, "He will love me more than old Dame Gothel does," and she said yes and laid her hand in his.

"I will gladly go away with you, but I don't know how to get down," she added. Bring a strand of silk with you every time you come, and I'll weave a ladder out of it. When that is completed, I will come down, and you will __transport__ me on your horse."

"You wicked child!" exclaimed the Witch. "What do you say!" I hear you say. I thought I'd __separated__ you from the rest of the world, but you've duped me!"

In her rage, she clutched Rapunzel's lovely locks, wrapped them twice around her left hand, grabbed a pair of __scissors__ with her right, and snip, snap, they were cut off, and the lovely braids lay on the ground.

However, on the same day that she cast out Rapunzel, the Witch, in the evening, glued the braids of hair she had __cut__ off to the window hook; and when the King's Son came and cried:

The King's Son climbed. He did not see his __beloved__ Rapunzel above but rather the Witch, who glared at him with wicked and cruel eyes.

He __escaped__ with his life, but the thorns he landed on punctured his eyes.

So he wandered around in misery for a few __years__ before arriving in the desert, where Rapunzel lived in misfortune. He heard a voice and went toward it because it sounded familiar. When he approached, Rapunzel recognized him and __sobbed__ on his neck. Two of her tears wetted his eyes, causing them to clear and allowing him to see as before.

He led her to his Kingdom, where he was joyfully received, and they lived __happily__ and merrily for a long time.

3rd Grade Geography Words

Instructions: Match the science words to the correct meaning.

1	L	Atlas	→	A collection of maps of the planet Earth.
2	A	Atoll	→	A coral reef or an island in the shape of a ring.
3	F	Altitude	→	The measure of elevation above sea level.
4	N	Border	→	An artificial line drawn segregating two geographical areas.
5	O	Capital	→	A city exercising primary status and where the government is located.
6	I	Country	→	A political state or a nation. For example, India, Thailand.
7	M	Desert	→	A large area covered with sand, where water or vegetation is either very little or not present at all.
8	G	Earth	→	The 3rd planet of our solar system and the planet in which we all live.
9	R	Equator	→	A line drawn on the center of the earth separating the north and south pole.
10	B	Geography	→	The study of the planet Earth's physical features.
11	K	Glacier	→	A mass of ice that is slowly moving.
12	D	Hemisphere	→	The half of a sphere. Hint: Northern and Southern____.
13	J	Latitude	→	The measure of the distance from the north or the south of the Equator.
14	E	Longitude	→	The measure of the distance from the east or the west of Prime Meridian.
15	S	Meridian	→	An imaginary circle passing through two poles.
16	Q	Plain	→	A piece of land that is flat.
17	P	Plateau	→	A piece of land on high ground.
18	H	Strait	→	A narrow passage of water connecting two water bodies.
19	C	Tributary	→	A stream that flows into a large lake, or a river.

3rd Grade Geography: Rivers

1. **Rivers vary in _____.**
    a. height
    b. size

2. **A river is a moving, flowing _____ of water.**
    a. body
    b. streams

3. **A river is a body of primarily _____ that flows across the land's surface.**
    a. freshwater
    b. biome

4. **When one stream meets another, they_____.**
    a. cross over
    b. merge

5. **When a river comes to an end, it's known as the _____.**
    a. mouth
    b. lake

6. **A large number of _____ form a river.**
    a. tributaries
    b. oceans

7. **A river expands as it _____ more and more water from its tributaries.**
    a. collects
    b. decreases

8. **The _____ runs for 4,135 miles.**
    a. Nile River
    b. Mississippi River

9. **_____ flows through several countries on the South American continent, including Brazil.**
    a. Amazon River
    b. Antarctica River

10. **_____ and _____ systems form the longest river system in North America.**
    a. Mississippi River and Missouri River
    b. Mississippi River and Michigan River

Extra Credit: Answer The Following 3 Questions: (1.) Where is majority of all water located on Earth? (2.) What is all the water on earth called? (3.) Why the Earth is called Blue planet?

NO ANSWERS- INDEPENDENT RESEARCH QUESTIONS

3rd Grade Science: Albert Einstein

Albert Einstein was born in __Germany__ on March 14, 1879. Because he was Jewish, he fled to the United States to avoid Hitler and the Second World War.

His father gave him a simple __pocket__ compass when he was about five years old, and it quickly became his favorite toy!

He developed an interest in __mathematics__ and science at the age of seven.

When Einstein was about ten years old, a much older friend gave him a large stack of science, mathematics, and philosophy __books__.

He'd published his first scientific __paper__ by the age of sixteen. That is absolutely incredible!

Numerous reports have shown that Einstein __failed__ math in school, but his family has stated that this is not the case. They claimed he was always at the __top__ of his class in math and could solve some challenging problems.

As an adult, he frequently __missed__ appointments, and because his mind was all over the place, his lectures were a little difficult to understand.

He didn't wear __socks__ and had uncombed hair! Even at posh dinners, he'd arrive unkempt, with crumpled clothes and, of course, no socks!

An __experiment__ in 1919 proved the theory correct. He became famous almost __overnight__, and he suddenly received invitations to travel worldwide, as well as honors from all over the world!

In 1921, he was awarded the __Nobel__ Prize for Physics. He'd come a long way from the boy who was told he'd never amount to anything!

Today, his other discoveries enabled us to have things like garage __door__ openers, televisions, and DVD players. Time magazine named him "Person of the Century" in 1999.

One of his favorite activities was to take a __boat__ out on a lake and take his notebook with him to think and write everything down. Perhaps this is what inspired him to create his inventions!

Einstein's first __marriage__ produced two sons. His daughter, Lierserl, is believed to have died when she was young. He married twice, and she died before him.

3rd Grade Science: All About Beavers

Beavers are mammals well-known for their **building** abilities.

Beavers are **rodents** , which are a type of animal.

Beavers are **slow** on land, but their webbed back feet help them swim.

Beavers are herbivores, which means they eat **plants** .

The beaver's large front teeth never stop **growing** .

Beavers have a translucent third eyelid (called a nictitating membrane) that covers and protects their

eyes while still allowing some sight **underwater** .

Even in the wee hours of the morning, Beavers have a hard time keeping their hands off the

 hammer .

Beavers will **slap** the water with their broad, scaly tail to warn other beavers in the area that a

predator is approaching.

However, due to hunting for its **fur** and glands for medicine, as well as the beavers' tree-felling and

damming affecting other land uses, the population has declined to around 12 million.

Beavers can live in the **wild** for up to 24 years.

Extra Credit: Answer These 3 questions: 1. Are beavers friendly? 2. Why are beavers' teeth orange? 3. How many beavers live in a dam?

[NO ANSWERS. INDEPENDENT RESEARCH.]

3rd Grade Science: Helium

1. **Helium is an ___, ___, and colorless gas at room temperature.**
   a. orderly, tasteful
   b. odorless, tasteless

2. **Helium is one of the ____ elements in the universe.**
   a. heaviest
   b. lightest

3. **Helium is classified as an inert or ____ gas.**
   a. noble
   b. odor

4. **____Pierre Janssen discovered helium for the first time in 1868.**
   a. Scientist
   b. Astronomer

5. **Helium is used to make ____ and airships float.**
   a. kites
   b. balloons

6. **The internal cores of ____ are constantly producing helium.**
   a. stars
   b. the sun

7. **Helium protects divers from being poisoned by too much ____.**
   a. oxygen
   b. gas

8. **Helium can be found trapped underground in ____ gas reservoirs as a result of radioactive decay.**
   a. natural
   b. minerals

Extra Credit: Answer The Following 3 Questions: 1. What is helium made from? 2. Can you make a balloon float without helium? 3. Why did my helium balloons sink overnight?

[NO ANSWERS. INDEPENDENT RESEARCH]

3rd Grade Life Skills: Internet Safety

Internet **safety** is the act of making one's self safer while surfing the web.

You may enjoy going online to watch **videos** , play games, and communicate with friends and family.

Because you are becoming more independent online and may go online **unsupervised** , you face more internet safety risks than younger children.

You **protect** yourself from potentially harmful or inappropriate content and activities when you take practical internet safety precautions.

1. Unless my parents have given me permission, I will not give out **personal** information such as my home address, phone number, or my parents' work address/phone number.

2. If I come across something that makes me **uncomfortable** , I will immediately notify my parents.

3. I will never **agree** to meet someone I "met" online without first discussing with my parents. If my parents agree to the meeting, I will make sure that it is held in a public location and bring a parent with me.

4. If my parents think a picture of me or someone else online is **inappropriate** , I will discuss the issue with them and refrain from posting it.

5. I will not respond to any **hurtful** messages or make me feel uncomfortable in any way. I don't believe that it is my fault if I receive such a message. If I do, I will immediately notify my parents.

6. Without their **permission** , I will not be able to access other areas or break these rules.

7. Other than my parents, I will not share my **passwords** with anyone else (even if they are my best friends).

8. I will consult with my parents before **downloading** or installing software or doing anything else that could potentially harm our computer or mobile device or that could compromise my family's privacy.

9. I will responsibly conduct myself on the internet, refraining from doing anything that is harmful to others or in **violation** of the law.

10. I will educate my parents on how I have fun and learn new **skills** online and teach them about the internet, computers, and other technology.

Extra Credit: Answer These 2 questions: 1. What is meant by Internet safety? 2. How can you stay safe on the Internet?

[NO ANSWERS. INDEPENDENT RESEARCH.]

3rd Grade Science: The First Moon Walk

On July 20, 1969, a record-breaking event occurred when millions of people gathered around their television sets to witness two American astronauts accomplish something no one had ever done before. Neil Armstrong and Edwin "Buzz" Aldrin became the first humans to walk on the moon, wearing bulky spacesuits and oxygen backpacks.

Armstrong famously said after the two stepped onto the lunar surface, "That's one small step for a man, one giant leap for mankind."

Russia launched the first artificial satellite, Sputnik 1, into space in 1957. Following that, the United States launched several satellites of its own. Both countries wanted to be the first to send a person into space.

It wasn't until 1961 that a person went into space: Russian Yuri Gagarin became the first on April 12, 1961. Alan Shepard of the United States became the first American in space less than a month later. Following these achievements, President John F. Kennedy challenged the National Aeronautics and Space Administration (NASA) to land a man on the moon in ten years or less.

NASA got right to work. On July 16, 1969, the Apollo 11 spacecraft was preparing to launch three astronauts into space.

As part of the selection process for the Apollo 11 astronauts, officials from NASA chose Neil Armstrong, Buzz Aldrin, and Michael Collins. The spacecraft approached the moon's surface just four days after taking off from Florida's Kennedy Space Center.

The three men separated before landing. Collins boarded Apollo 11's command module, the Columbia, from which he would remain in lunar orbit. Armstrong and Aldrin boarded the Eagle, Apollo 11's lunar module, and began their descent to the moon's surface.

The Eagle made a daring landing in a shallow moon crater known as the Sea of Tranquility, which was a risky move. Most people who watched the landing on television were unaware that the Eagle had only 20 seconds of landing fuel remaining at this point in the flight.

1. Neil _____ and Edwin "Buzz" ____ became the first humans to walk on the moon.
   a. Armstrong and Aldrin
   b. Armadale and Aladdin

2. Russia launched the first artificial satellite called ____.
   a. Spank 1.0
   b. Sputnik 1

3. The Eagle made a daring landing in a shallow moon crater known as the ____.
   a. Sea of Tranquility
   b. U.S.A Sea of Trinity

4. On ____, the Apollo 11 spacecraft was preparing to launch three astronauts into space.
   a. July 16, 1989
   b. July 16, 1969

5. Russian _____ became the first person in space on April 12, 1961
   a. Yuri Gagarin
   b. Yari Kim Jun

6. Armstrong and Aldrin boarded the ____, Apollo 11's lunar module, and began their descent to the moon's surface.
   a. Eagle
   b. Black Bird

3rd Grade Science: The First Moon Walk Part II

1. **NASA is currently working on sending humans to another planet: _____.**

   a. Saturn

   b. Mars

2. **On _____, the Apollo 11 crew returned to Earth.**

   a. July 24, 1969

   b. July 25, 1967

3. **The _____ is a space research station.**

   a. US International Center Moon

   b. International Space Station

4. **Armstrong took the lead as mission _____ and became the first person to set foot on the moon.**

   a. commander

   b. scientist

5. **The astronauts saw a _____ reading that stated they "came in peace for all mankind,".**

   a. written letter

   b. plaque

6. **The last moon mission took place in _____.**

   a. 1972

   b. 1975

Extra Credit: Answer The Following 3 Questions: 1. How old was Neil Armstrong when he landed on the moon? 2. Is the flag still on the moon? 3. What was the first animal in space?

[No Answers. Independent Reseach]

3rd Grade Art Words

1	D	Contrast	→	Use of opposites near or beside one another (light and dark, rough and smooth)
2	B	Composition	→	The arrangement of forms in a work of art.
3	N	Cool colors	→	Mostly green, blue, violet (purple).
4	P	Hue	→	The name of a color – red blue, yellow, etc.
5	K	Intensity	→	Brightness of a color.
6	H, M	Texture	→	Refers to the way things feel or look as though they might feel if they were touched.
7	I	Subject matter	→	The topic of interest or the primary theme of an artwork.
8	L	Tint	→	Light values of a color (adding white)
9	E	Shade	→	The dark values of a color (adding black).
10	F	Warm colors	→	Red, orange, yellow.
11	J	Variety	→	Principle of design concerned with difference or contrast.
12	G	Focal point	→	The center of interest of an artwork; the part you look at first.
13	O	Line	→	A mark with greater length than width.
14	A	Shape	→	A closed line.
15	C	Space	→	The area between and around objects.
16	M, H	Texture	→	The surface quality that can be seen and felt.

Extra Credit Question: What are the elements of art? List each of them with a description.

INDEPENDENT RESEARCH

3rd Grade Music: The Orchestra
Vocabulary Words

Who wants to attend an orchestral performance? Obviously, you do! Orchestras are fantastic. An orchestra, at its most basic, is a large musical ensemble. Traditional orchestras have sections for woodwind, brass, strings, and percussion instruments.

The orchestra as we know it today originated in the early 1600s. Instruments were added and removed over the next several centuries, and what we now call the modern orchestra began to take shape. Violins became the orchestra's primary string instrument in the 17th century. More woodwind instruments were added over time, and by the 18th century, French horns, trombones, and trumpets were commonplace.

Throughout the 17th century, orchestras were small, with only about 18-20 members, and the composer was often a performer, often on the harpsichord or violin. As a result, there was no real director. In the 18th century, composers like Johann Sebastian Bach and Wolfgang Amadeus Mozart made orchestral music famous and influential, inspiring kings and peasants alike. During this period, concert performance indeed became a respected profession.

Ludwig van Beethoven, a 19th-century composer who standardized the orchestra using pairs of each woodwind and brass instrument, took the next big step. Beethoven composed works that made full use of the entire range of instruments, from high to low, and gave each section more critical roles, rather than letting the strings carry the majority of the melody on their own.

_____

Unscramble the names of the instruments found in the orchestra.

woodwind	cello	xylophone	violin	piano	trumpet
drums	oboe	brass	trombone	flute	clarinet
percussion	conductor	saxophone	harp		

1. tulef   f l u t e

2. involi   v i o l i n

3. eoob   o b o e

4. articlne   c l a r i n e t

5. srudm   d r u m s

6. ddnwoiwo   w o o d w i n d

7. rbass   b r a s s

8. uniocrspse   p e r c u s s i o n

9. lceol   c e l l o

10. ahrp   h a r p

11. erpttum   t r u m p e t

12. rootmebn   t r o m b o n e

13. enlhoxypo   x y l o p h o n e

14. udcootrnc   c o n d u c t o r

15. oniap   p i a n o

16. heonoasxp   s a x o p h o n e

ADDITIONAL ASSIGNMENTS PLANNER

○ MONDAY

GOALS THIS WEEK

_____
_____
_____
_____
_____
_____
_____

○ TUESDAY

○ WEDNESDAY

WHAT TO STUDY

_____
_____
_____
_____
_____
_____

○ THURSDAY

_____
_____
_____
_____

○ FRIDAY

_____
_____
_____

EXTRA CREDIT WEEKEND WORK
○ SATURDAY / SUNDAY

_____
_____
_____

ADDITIONAL ASSIGNMENTS PLANNER

○ MONDAY

○ TUESDAY

○ WEDNESDAY

○ THURSDAY

○ FRIDAY

EXTRA CREDIT WEEKEND WORK
○ SATURDAY / SUNDAY

GOALS THIS WEEK

WHAT TO STUDY

ADDITIONAL ASSIGNMENTS PLANNER

○ MONDAY

GOALS THIS WEEK

_____

_____

○ TUESDAY

_____

_____

_____

○ WEDNESDAY

_____

WHAT TO STUDY

_____

_____

○ THURSDAY

_____

_____

_____

○ FRIDAY

_____

_____

_____

EXTRA CREDIT WEEKEND WORK
○ SATURDAY / SUNDAY

_____

_____

_____

_____

ADDITIONAL ASSIGNMENTS PLANNER

○ MONDAY

GOALS THIS WEEK

○ TUESDAY

○ WEDNESDAY

WHAT TO STUDY

○ THURSDAY

○ FRIDAY

EXTRA CREDIT WEEKEND WORK
○ SATURDAY / SUNDAY

GRADES TRACKER

Week	Monday	Tuesday	Wednesday	Thursday	Friday
1					
2					
3					
4					
5					
6					
7					
8					
9					
10					
11					
12					
13					
14					
15					
16					
17					
18					

Notes

GRADES TRACKER

Week	Monday	Tuesday	Wednesday	Thursday	Friday
1					
2					
3					
4					
5					
6					
7					
8					
9					
10					
11					
12					
13					
14					
15					
16					
17					
18					

Notes

End of the Year Evaluation

Name: _____

Grade/Level: _____ Date: _____

Subjects Studied: _____
_____
_____

Cut out book

Goals Accomplished: _____
_____
_____
_____

Most Improved Areas: _____
_____
_____
_____

Areas of Improvement: _____
_____
_____

Main Curriculum Evaluation	Satisfied		Final Grades
_____	Yes	No	A= Above Standards
_____	Yes	No	S= Meets Standards
_____	Yes	No	N= Needs Improvement

A= Above Standards
S= Meets Standards
N= Needs Improvement
98-100 A+
93-97 A
90-92 A
88-89 B+
83-87 B
80-82 B
78-79 C+
73-77 C
70-72 C
68-69 D+
62-67 D
60-62 D
59 & Below F

_____ Yes No

_____ Yes No

_____ Yes No

_____ Yes No

_____ Yes No

_____ Yes No

Final Grades
_____
_____
_____
_____
_____
_____

Most Enjoyed: _____
_____

Least Enjoyed: _____
_____

Made in United States
North Haven, CT
11 March 2023

33911861R00064